go out in joy !

go out in joy!

NINA HERRMANN

JOHN KNOX PRESS
ATLANTA

Library of Congress Cataloging in Publication Data

Herrmann, Nina, 1943–
    Go out in joy!

    1. Herrmann, Nina, 1943–   2. Chaplains, Hospital
-Illinois-Chicago-Biography.   3. Chicago-Biography.
4. Sick children. I. Title.
II. BV4335.H38   248'.2'0924 [B]   76–449–72
ISBN 0–8042–2073–5

© 1977 John Knox Press
Second Printing 1977
Printed in the United States of America

to my parents
with abiding love

and to the varig spirit,
in whose moments is the dawn

for you shall go out in joy,
and be led forth in peace;
the mountains and the hills before you
shall break forth into singing,
and all the trees of the field
shall clap their hands.

ISAIAH 55:12

acknowledgments

This book was not written to be a book. It was written to tell my divinity school professors what it was like to be an embryo hospital chaplain who had never faced suffering and death. It was to fulfill a requirement . . . but mostly it was the paper-and-pencil process of one person trying to unscramble a compression of feelings, thoughts, reactions, and questions.

That it evolved, basically in its original form, into a book is the result of Dr. Martin E. Marty of the University of Chicago: my adviser, good friend—and agent! To him my deep thanks, not only for his literary encouragement but for his support and kindness throughout my divinity school days and beyond.

Many thanks, too, to Dr. Martin Maloney of Northwestern University, who, by giving me *freedom* of pen and mind in my undergraduate days, helped me discover the *fun* of writing.

To watch your child die or struggle daily with a physical or mental handicap is a pain that is not describable. But each of us has a neighbor somewhere who is either sinking or swimming within this pain. If these writings do nothing else, perhaps they will contribute to the sensitivity of the persons who read them—the sensitivity that encourages one to reach out and touch, life to life, another person who may be terminally ill or physically or mentally handicapped, or have a child who is.

The people in this book are real. Care has been taken to protect their identities and privacy. But they need no apologies. They are truly valiant people—children, parents, nurses, doctors, relatives, and friends—who endured. To them I give my unspeakably deep appreciation always. For this book is *their* gift to you.

. . . Their gift, and the gift of Dr. Elam Davies, Pastor of the Fourth Presbyterian Church in Chicago, who—though consistently warning me of the "hazards" of ministry—has given me my greatest spiritual and personal strength and support throughout. His theology is uniquely uplifting and worthy. It is neither panacea nor condemnation. It is affirmative of the worth of personhood . . . it is inclusive rather than exclusive . . . and it reminds—at times when one is at the brink of despair —that God's love is unconditional and everlasting and will conquer all in the end. To him I owe whatever good I have been or am able to be as minister, no matter how far the journey takes me.

Nina Herrmann
Chicago, 1976

prologue

There's an interim now, a lull before the storm, a waiting for the other shoe to drop . . . what you will.

Nine-year-old Riann Miles is going to die, probably before summer. No one can be sure. But she has begun her final descent. There is no way back.

Right now she is still "with it." She still laughs and smiles and wrinkles up her nose, and giggles, and plays little jokes, and complains when she has to take her afternoon "rest." She still hugs and kisses and gives back love.

I want to remember her this way. Desperately I want to remember her this way. But it won't happen. The slides that stack up in my mind and play back at random years after their scenes were live will include pictures of Riann breathing beyond laughter and love. I know now the slides will be there. But I do not know now what they will look like. And that's what frightens me.

Yet, I have seen other children die—both in the moment and in the months. So why is Riann different? I'm not sure. Maybe it's because I have known her long enough and well enough that my love for her is being returned beyond just a moment of sharing . . . And that forebodes the difference between sympathetic loss and personal loss when the days beyond love returned come.

But let me tell you the story from the beginning. I did not keep a diary. A good journalist would have kept a diary. But I have not lived these months as a journalist. So you will have only my random slides reached for. Perhaps some will not return. Perhaps that is a kindness.

1.

It was a wet day in October and I was in bed with a box of Kleenex and a bottle of cold pills.

One month earlier I had resigned from my job, effective December 31. I was a reporter for a large Midwest television station. It was a goal I had had since my last year in college. For the first two years after the goal had been reached, I was ecstatic. I loved every moment of my work: the people I met, the conversations I had, the places I saw. I touched many forms of living, of existing. I was allowed to be creative, to reach into the emotions, the pain, the joy—the humanness beyond the "hard" news.

Then all that stopped: new management, save money, new approach . . . Sellout; that's what I saw happening, anyway. It wasn't the same. Now I was simply taking home a paycheck—a *big* paycheck, but only that.

Maybe I saw it coming. I don't know. But for some reason or another two autumns earlier I had enrolled in divinity school. For two years and one quarter I both went to school and worked, never sure why I was going to school. I think I chose ministry because I admire my minister, Dr. Elam Davies. Maybe if I had admired a physician I'd have studied medicine, or an attorney I'd have studied law. Maybe that's all there was to it. I've always been impressionable.

Be that as it may, as I sat in bed that wet October day with my box of Kleenex I was trying to decide what to do with myself after my television news job ended in December.

The coursework for my master's degree in divinity was out of the way, or would be if I passed the two courses I was taking that fall. So after December I wouldn't have to attend classes and I also wouldn't have to work. I had saved enough money to live for five months without a job. I'd be "free" until June.

Sometime during those five months I did want to finish my master's paper and take my oral exam so I could get my degree. But I really had no plans to take up a form of ministry beyond that. Besides, that was too far away. The immediate problem was January through May.

I debated spending a month at home with my parents. But I decided we'd drive each other crazy. It was too long. They love me and I them. But they were too upset that at twenty-eight I was quitting my "well-paying" reporting job. They wanted things in my life settled—like marriage, security, children. Especially since I'm an only child; all their eggs in one basket, that kind of thing. I wanted that too, mind you. But it hadn't happened, and I now spent only a moderate amount of time worrying about it.

No, home for more than two weeks at Christmas was out.

Europe? Yes, that was for sure. But I don't ski, so springtime was best. I didn't want to spend all five months over there; too expensive. No, I'd just do Europe in April and May, maybe get my master's paper written on some hills in Switzerland. That sounded nice!

So what about January through March? Blank. I blew my nose and was about to give up the heavy pondering and take a nap. Clinical Pastoral Education! That was a possibility, a good possibility. Somewhere I had the pamphlet. I threw off the covers.

Part of my divinity school training required one quarter of Clinical Pastoral Education (C.P.E.). This, at best, is a full-time job, five days a week, working in a hospital as a student chaplain . . . for twelve weeks. That's what I would do between January and March! Get my Clinical Pastoral Education out of the way.

I found the folder under my bed in a box. There were a number of hospitals in the area offering C.P.E. I decided to look for one within reasonable distance of my apartment, and offering a stipend. Why not? Better money than no money. That certainly narrowed the choice—to one: University Adult and Children's Hospital Center, a combined program working both with adults and children.

I telephoned. Today was the last day for applications, I was told. The tone of the voice implied "sorry."

"I'm in bed with a cold," I pleaded. "But I won't breathe on the chaplain if he'll just see me for an interview."

"Wait a minute, please."

I waited.

"OK," said the voice. "But don't come in today. He'll extend the time and see you in two days."

"Thank you very much," I said. "Good-bye."

Somehow I figured his secretary had put in a good word for me, though I wasn't sure why. She had. " 'Cause you're a girl," she explained later. "I figured they needed some more girls in the chaplain program!"

Her "good word" was to change my life for a time . . .

Maybe it was because I looked different—so different from the average student chaplain that I figured the chaplain-director's curiosity would beat the odds against me. But whatever the reason, right then on that wet October afternoon I figured he'd accept me. It wasn't being sure of myself. It was just knowing how people had reacted to me in the past.

I was right. He accepted me. I received the letter November first.

So it was decided: Clinical Pastoral Education from January through March, Europe from April until June, some job or another after that . . .

I didn't think anything more about it, just saved my money.

2.

I had never seen anyone die, never been around
death or serious illness. I wasn't afraid of it, but I didn't really
know for sure what to be afraid of.

When I would tell people what I was going to do in January
I'd mouth the words "be a hospital chaplain." But I didn't feel
anything like fear of death and dying. I had no associations I could
make.

As I was dressing on the morning of my first day, January 2,
I had a feeling of unreality, of dissociation. It was as if I was
watching a stranger dress, tell the cab driver "University Hospital
Center," and walk up those stairs to the second floor rooms of the
Clinical Pastoral Education office.

"This isn't for real," I wanted to say to someone. "It surely isn't
television news reporting; and that's all I've lived since college."

The C.P.E. offices were in an old building several doors away
from Children's and about two blocks away from Adult. There
were several small rooms, all somewhat dilapidated. I had seen
them when I came for my interview. But now they belonged to
my life; my inspection was closer. I was actually going to come
to these offices and have seminars with other students and the
adviser every weekday for the next twelve weeks? Me? Who had
never spent more than two hours in the same place on any work-
day in the last four years? Who had interviewed presidents and
senators and movie stars and business leaders and authors and
crooked politicians and honest politicians . . . Yes, and protesters
and fire victims and welfare recipients and unionists and murder-
ers and thieves . . . And almost every other kind of person I had

figured one time over coffee. Me? Here? For three months?
Did I feel like it was a game?

No; but it's hard to say all that and leave you with the real
feeling I had in the moments I walked up those stairs and into
those rooms. It wasn't one of haughty incredulity, though that's
how my words may sound. And it wasn't one of wanting to turn
back. Never, not once, have I had that feeling. It was just one of
blank-association: I had a hat, but it just didn't seem to match my
outfit and I couldn't visualize a nail to hang it on. I was ready,
but for what I didn't know.

As it turned out, I was early. It was 9 A.M. and I should have
been there at 9:30. The chaplain, Craig Hatfield, was there. "We
usually have coffee," he said, "but I can't find the grounds." He
had brown curly hair and corduroy clothes. He sat sort of rum-
pled.

"Is there a coffee shop nearby?" I offered. "I'll get some."

"Yeah, 'cross the street."

I went. Returned with four cups, two extra. "Gotta stop spending my money," I reminded myself. "It's only going out now!"

Homer Lowden, another student, was there when I returned.
He was from the Methodist seminary down the street. He was
average-looking, moustache, blond hair, glasses. He seemed
friendly.

A few minutes later three more men came in. Terry Greer,
skinny, medium height, black hair, southern accent. Al O'Connor, tall, good-looking, young, brown hair, light complexion, steel-
rimmed glasses. And Ted Marshall, shorter, dark hair, jutting
chin, good-looking. All three were Catholic seminarians.

We did the usual "getting to know you" things. I didn't feel
uncomfortable. I didn't feel anything particular. It was still too
new.

That afternoon we toured the hospitals. Children's first, then
Adult. It's a good bit for one day but it goes too fast to guarantee
the validity of impressions. The only thing I remembered about
Children's was that I hoped I would get assigned to a new wing

—I always liked things clean and fresh—and that I would get a floor with older children on it so I wouldn't have to talk with parents as much. One floor in the old wing seemed to have nothing but babies. I didn't want that!

Children's seemed more threatening; Adult more like things I had already seen in my life. An old lady I used to visit for my church had died in Adult. They seemed to take good care of her.

We ended our day in a machine lunchroom at Adult, just to have some coffee and talk.

Wednesday we met some social workers at Adult and talked among ourselves. It seems like we may have seen a movie, but I don't remember for sure. Funny how being new at something strips you of everyday securities, like knowing where the ladies' room is and where to be alone for a minute . . . and who to trust. You just have to avoid drinking a lot of liquids and punt, I guess.

Thursday afternoon we got our floor assignments. I got a new wing at Adult; I think it was the same floor my old lady friend had died on. But at Children's I got the old wing with all the babies—just the one I didn't want! You can't win them all, I guess.

I went to Adult first that Friday. It seemed safer. And it was nearly three-thirty by the time I braved Children's. I looked for the head nurse, Mary Cooke, and introduced myself as the new student chaplain.

"I heard we were going to have a woman," she said; "Good! You came at the right time, too," she added. "I'm about ready to give report so I can't talk with you now. But the doctors are making rounds. Why don't I introduce you to them and you can go along. That will give you a fast picture of the whole floor."

I can't tell you how *new* all this was! I didn't know what "rounds" were, or what "report" was. I had the gut feeling that I'd really rather *not* see the whole floor at once. But I had no choice, I figured.

Mrs. Cooke and I entered a large room with four cribs. At the far end of the room on the right side stood about six doctors in hospital coats. One was washing his hands, another was raising the side of a crib.

Mrs. Cooke waited for a between-sentences, interrupted to introduce me, and left. The doctors looked, nodded, gave professional half-smiles. The one washing his hands made a slight oriental bow. I thought it was a bit weird. Then they went on with their rounds. Mrs. Cooke had introduced two or three doctors by name, but I didn't remember.

The patients were all babies or toddlers. All! Not one I could really talk with. I followed the doctors in and out of rooms. Most had four beds, most were filled with patients.

I heard medical language. I saw children with bandages wrapped around their heads. Some had tubes implanted. Two babies were lying on their stomachs on boards. One had a big bandage on his back. The other had a big open wound—like an oozing mountain—on her back. It wasn't easy to look. I didn't. I had no idea what was wrong with the baby.

Sometimes the doctors would walk by a crib and not stop. Why, I wondered? They took off bandages and looked at wounds. They talked and talked and talked. I was trying to keep my head above water. I didn't understand any of it. No one was there to explain. I just stood back out of everyone's way, trying to fade into the wall and look interested at the same time.

But I could barely look at all. When they'd uncover a wound, I'd look in that direction, but I would blur my eyes so I really couldn't see. My feet hurt, too.

One baby had four scars on her head—one in each "corner." She had been beaten by one of her parents somebody said. Why four symmetrical scars, I wondered? Was it the beating, or an operation? Would I have to talk with those parents?

On and on went the doctors. I followed and waited and half-watched and listened to words I didn't understand. It was getting hotter and hotter. I didn't know if it was me or the ward.

It was me. We had been in a lot of rooms. This was Bobby's room. He had a bandage on his head. They unwrapped it and unwrapped it, like a turban. Bobby was really cute, about one year old. He had four scars on his head. Just like the other baby. They thought one of his parents had beaten him, too. Was that the kind of operation they did on children who were beaten? Four scars?

The room started to spin. I got big black and yellow spots in front of my eyes. I knew what that meant: Fainting.

I was very hot. I turned and quietly left Bobby's room. I was operating by radar, fighting like mad to keep my faculties long enough to find a ladies' room. That's the misery of being "new." Where's the ladies' room? I didn't have enough stamina to ask; I was almost gone. The hall was spinning faster and faster.

There it was: "Ladies." I went in. It was a self-contained little room. Thank goodness! I locked the door, threw down the toilet seat, sat, put my head way down, and held on. I know I didn't move for five minutes.

But I didn't faint.

Finally, I put up my head, and sat and sat and sat. I didn't think. I didn't feel. I just breathed.

At last I got up, splashed cold water on my face, opened the door and walked back down the hall. I wasn't exactly sure I was going in the right direction. But I came to Bobby's room, and the doctors were still there! (As I said, they took a long time with each patient.) I slipped in quietly, trying not to be noticed.

The last thing I remember about that day was the doctor who had given me the little bow of greeting earlier. He looked up at me now over the tops of his half-glasses as if to say, "Well, look who came back. I wondered if you would." It was brief. He didn't say a word. But it made me feel good. I guess I knew then that I wouldn't quit.

3.

Terry Greer had volunteered to be the student chaplain on call that first weekend. So I and the rest of the students had Saturday and Sunday off. I decided Saturday morning that since I was going to *have* to talk with parents—because there seemed to be only "babies" on my floor at Children's—as well as talk with adult patients at Adult, I had better get something to make people take me seriously, something to make them recognize me as a chaplain, something like . . . a clerical collar.

I got out the yellow pages. I didn't know much about clerical garb. I finally found a store that was open on Saturday, but I didn't know how to get to it on public transportation. And there was no way I was going to pay for a cab any more!

David, good old David and his Mercedes! I had been dating David off and on for nearly five years. He was forty-four, had never married, and likely wouldn't until he needed a nurse. He dated as many girls as he could. But I was the only one he had dated for any length of time. I was still a challenge, they weren't.

I had figured David out a long time ago. He knew I dated other men, too. But he was *sure* none of them could be as wealthy or desirable as he!

Anyway, David had a blue Mercedes convertible. He let me drive it. It wasn't that new, but I loved it, especially the eight-track stereo with four speakers.

It was raining when I arrived at the clerical goods store on North Hamilton. It reminded me of a dry goods store my grandfather had owned. I fancied that I heard a bell jingle as I opened the door.

Inside were long rows of wooden and glass cases, shelves piled high with books and boxes, and a row of hanging choir and clerical robes on the far side of the room.

Two gray-haired salesladies were chatting behind an old-fashioned metal cash register. "May I help you?" asked the shorter one.

"Yes, thank you. I'd like a clerical collar."

"What size?"

"I don't know. I guess you'll have to measure."

Silence.

"Is it for you?"

"Yes."

"Oh, I see. Well, I don't know if we have one that small. They only make them in men's sizes." Pause. "I don't know why, with more women coming into the ministry these days. But I guess that's just the way it is."

She pulled the tape measure from around my neck. "Thirteen and a half. We don't have one that small. Are you going to wear it with a robe? If so, maybe one of our white lace choir robe collars would do?"

"No, I'm going to wear it with a dress."

"Oh. Well, we just don't have one that small. We could order it, but it would take about four weeks. We do have a fourteen, maybe a half inch wouldn't make that much difference."

"All right. May I try that?"

"It looks all right. You really can't tell, I mean about the half inch. How does it feel?"

That little old lady had no way of knowing what feelings and unfeelings were going through me then. I had never put on a clerical collar before. It was the kind of thing I hadn't planned to do until I was ordained. But at the same time, it was something I had wanted to do ever since I had started divinity school.

I suppose to anyone else—to the little old ladies, perhaps—the collar really looked weird. But to me, it was me. I wasn't a character in a play. I wasn't acting a role. I didn't look weird to me.

"It feels fine. A bit loose, but that's all right. I need it now."

"Do you want me to order a thirteen and a half?"

"No, thank you. I'll only need it for twelve weeks."

"Oh, I see."

She didn't see. I suddenly realized that. I must have been quite a mystery to the two old ladies. I hadn't really thought of that.

"If you'll tell me the name of the church where you work we can give you a ten percent clerical discount. But I must have the name of the church . . ."

"Well, I'm really not affiliated in that way with a church."

Looks exchanged between the two old ladies.

"I'm a student chaplain at University Children's and Adult Hospitals. I started this week and I'll be there through March."

"Oh! That must be interesting!" Fluttered relief, not a "Jesus freak" after all.

"I guess so. I'm still sort of new."

"Do you have trouble . . . I mean, being a woman?"

"Not so far, but that's why I want the collar: Identity." (A crutch I wondered?)

"Yes, I guess that would be a problem. Well, good luck. Enjoy your collar. If you want a thirteen and a half, just call, we'll order it."

"Thank you."

Jingle. Jingle. Back to the Mercedes. Back to David.

"Well, let's see. Man, that's weird. Don't wear it when we go out, you'll ruin my reputation! Grief! Giving up a glamor job like yours to run around in that thing and take care of sick kids. You'll be sorry! Why couldn't you just have volunteered on Saturdays?"

It was the same speech I had heard before and before and would hear again and again. David's bark is always worse than his bite. I can count on him in a pinch, and that's what matters.

Barbecued ribs and martinis. The collar stayed in its box.

Later, alone, at home, I tried on the collar with every hairdo and outfit I could think of at the moment. Who would know? I'm still a woman, after all.

4.

Monday morning we talked about the weekend. Terry Greer waxed eloquent, sort of. He had had a weekend of saved souls, and on top of that, no one had died.

They all seemed so young, the other students. I hadn't done much "group" work. I can remember when first at divinity school I thought a "T" group was a gathering in which people sat around drinking tea and eating cookies! Groups had never been my thing. And after all was said and done, they still weren't to be.

I don't remember much of Monday afternoon. I guess I went over to Adult for a while. I was "on call" that evening. I wore my collar for the first time that day. Maybe it was getting used to it that made me forget everything else . . .

Until ten-thirty that night, that is.

We had been told by Craig Hatfield that when we were on call we should check with the nursing stations on each floor before going home, to see if there were any serious situations for which we might be called back. I did, and there weren't any until I reached the last station—six-center, Intensive Care—at Children's.

"There's a baby who will die within the next two hours," I was told. "She's a newborn, brought here from Plainfield at noon, lung problem. Her father and grandmother are in the waiting room. Her name is Tracy Marks."

"You're *sure* she's going to die? Tonight?"

"I'm sure."

The nurse was nice. She sensed I was new.

It had all been OK until now. Now it wasn't OK any more. A baby was going to die. She wouldn't wait until morning.

(Can't you keep her alive until tomorrow, until Ted Marshall, whose floor this is, gets here. I don't want to hear what you're saying. Let's just pretend you didn't . . .)

But she wouldn't wait until morning. She was going to die now. I had to talk with her father. The nurse was watching. She would know if I ran away home. I had to.

I didn't even know these people.

It seems like I took the long way around to the six-center waiting room. Maybe I didn't, because I wouldn't have known the long way then. Maybe I just walked slowly. Whatever . . . I finally got there.

They were over in the far right corner. Huddled. Much later I was to realize that parents of dying children always sit huddled. Maybe it's to keep themselves from exploding. Maybe it's to shelter against the blow. Maybe it's because their stomachs are too knotted for them to sit straight.

When I saw their faces I realized the negative effect a clerical collar can have in a situation like that. They thought the infant already had died, and I was sent to tell the news.

"I'm the chaplain on call," I explained, still standing. "I was just passing. Would you like to talk?"

"Oh, then you don't know anything," said the young man sitting on an orange vinyl stool.

I shook my head.

"He didn't mean it the way it sounded," said the lady. "It's just that his little daughter—newborn—is in the Intensive Care room and she's not doing too good. He saw you and thought . . ."

"I'm sorry," I said. "I didn't mean to frighten you. I'm afraid I don't have any news about your daughter," I lied.

"Won't you have a seat?" asked the lady. "I'm Sylvia Liskin and this is my son-in-law, Tony Marks."

The young man stood briefly and nodded as I sat down and introduced myself.

"You see," said the woman, "Tony and his wife, Mary, they

had another little girl die at birth two years ago, some of these same symptoms. The doctors said it wasn't genetic . . . wouldn't happen again . . ."

I don't remember whether I mentioned praying first or they did. But I think it was me. And that's what we did next. I knew the baby was going to die. They didn't. They had been waiting since noon. They wanted to hear words of hope, of life . . .

I had never lived through anything like this before. Never. The collar, the title chaplain, the whole bag full of symbols. Entering the lives of strangers—total strangers—at the close personal moment of death. It isn't a very real thing . . . at first.

In the moment I had to decide what was central. Was it me, the reverend figure, the holy intercessor? Was it the parents, frightened, separated by distance, suffering in a time set aside for rejoicing? Was it the baby, the little bundle of warmth soon to turn cold; the baby I hadn't even seen? One day I would discover it isn't any of these. And yet it is all of these.

That night I opted for "b"—the parents. As for "a"—me, even if I wanted to play the role, I didn't know how. I felt powerless to effect the change these people wanted. And it never entered my mind that the doctors could be wrong, to pray for a miracle, that the child had a chance to live. Was I just too rational a being, having already been told the answer was death? Had I "too little faith"? As for "c"—the child, there was nothing I could do to save her medically. And nothing within me was *afraid* to let her die, afraid that she would be alone, unloved.

But then, I never carried her, never bore her.

"Dear God . . ."

I don't remember what I said. I could make up something. I won't. I do know I didn't give up hope. I do know I prayed that little Tracy would live. But I also know that I prayed for acceptance in the face of God's greater knowledge and love that wants what's best for each of us, regardless of our own lack of understanding.

I also know that the corn on the little toe of my left foot hurt viciously the whole way through the prayer. When I look back on that night, the pain in that little toe is one of the vivid memories. Maybe because it was the only thing that seemed real, the only thing that I had experienced before, that I could latch onto . . .

But my most vivid memory is that of Tony Marks crying when he was told Tracy had died.

He had gotten up to pace, to be alone, to remind himself that he was alive.

It was hard for me to be sure they wanted me to stay. But they had kept talking, initiating sentences.

When Tony Marks was out of earshot and I was getting up to leave for a bit, the older woman beckoned me closer. "I know what's bothering Tony," she said. "He hasn't been going to church much lately, and he thinks this is God's way of punishing him."

How can people think God is like that, I thought to myself. And then I remembered a time when I had believed God was exactly like that!

"Under the circumstances," I said, "I can understand him feeling that way. But the God I believe in isn't like that. If God went around punishing everyone in exact measure for his sins, there wouldn't be any happiness or love in the world at all."

"I agree with you," said the woman. "And I've told Tony that. But maybe it would help if you told him. I mean, being a chaplain and all . . ."

That was the first time I realized anyone could take more seriously what I say because I wear a reversed collar and carry a title. It made me worry a lot more about the validity of what I say. It still does.

I never had a chance to talk with Tony Marks about his fears. While he was pacing, the doctor told him Tracy had died.

I remember his eyes as he walked back toward us. But no words will describe them. Then he wept . . . trying not to.

"She just didn't make it. She just didn't have the strength. Her little lungs were too weak," he repeated and repeated and repeated, choking. Would I pray again, please? This time he asked.

"Dear God . . ."

He sobbed. From the first words of the prayer throughout. It all burst out on the brown carpet and orange vinyl chairs. It was too personal for me to see.

From that night on, I have held those moments of raping grief at death in the highest respect and awe—as the total awareness of finitude. For never, never are we more human.

That was the climax, for me at least. I couldn't deal with anything more. More happened, and I remember participating in it, but not as something lived through, only as something watched.

Would I go with them to see the baby? To say good-bye, they asked.

Yes.

She was in an incubator. The top was tilted back. She was like a sleeping doll. They looked a long time. The father kissed her and stroked her little cheek . . . and wept. The grandmother wept. I stood there. She's asleep, that's all. I knew better. But she didn't look dead, just asleep. I had seen a sleeping baby before. I hadn't seen a dead baby before.

The doctor asked for permission for an autopsy, "to help future children and parents." They all say that. They have to say something. And it's important, the autopsy. But there's no way to wrap the words in cotton.

Would I take them to "admitting"—how funny the name sounded under the circumstances—to sign the "body release" papers, asked the nurse.

Yes.

It was after midnight. There was a young girl behind a small desk and this was probably all the excitement she would get all night. Or maybe it was an interruption in her daydreaming. Or maybe she was just uptight in the situation, too. Whatever it was, she didn't sound very sympathetic. She flew questions like darts: "Child's full name, parents' names, date of birth, time of birth, brothers' and sisters' names, name of funeral home to which the body is to be released . . ."

That last one got Tony Marks. He turned absolutely white. They discussed, he and his mother-in-law, and gave a name.

"If you change your mind on that," said the insipid girl, "call. That's all. Thank you."

I'm sorry. She didn't even say "I'm sorry." Maybe Tony Marks and his mother-in-law didn't notice, wouldn't have heard if she did say it.

But I needed it.

"Thank you," they said to me. "Thank you for staying."

"I'm sorry," I said. "Will you be all right getting home?"

"Yes . . .

"She lived twelve hours," said Tony Marks, not to anyone particular. "That's two hours longer than her sister. We've had twenty-two hours' worth of babies . . . almost a full day . . ."

They walked out the Emergency Room double doors. The cold air blasted in. They didn't turn back.

I think I went somewhere and sat down. But I don't remember.

5.

Tuesday I told the "group" about Tracy Marks.
They sympathized appropriately. But I couldn't tell it well. I felt
uncomfortable force-dissecting an experience that personal, that
new. It's difficult even now. Then it was impossible.

Craig Hatfield had wanted me to say what I felt when I still
was having trouble comprehending feeling itself. Perhaps people
can't say what they feel when they're in shock. And I guess I still
was, though I didn't know it then.

Early Tuesday evening I found Lindsay Grice. I had thought
she was a boy. Not because her name was Lindsay, but because
she had a crew cut.

Three-north, I was discovering, was the neurosurgery floor—
that's brain surgery. And that's why most of the patients had
bandages on their heads, all over their heads. And underneath the
bandages was . . . no hair.

Mrs. Cooke had suggested that I play with Lindsay. "She's
been in and out so many times in her four years that she needs
as much love and cuddling as she can get."

When I saw Lindsay I was apprehensive . . . for about two
minutes. On the left side of her head, a little toward the back,
was a square bandage. On the right side of her head, showing
through the crew cut, was a snakelike scar. I had never seen one
like it. It seemed to wind round and round. It had healed, so it
couldn't have been done recently, I reasoned. Her eyes were
crossed and she was skinny, skinny, and she couldn't stand up.

But she won. She beat out all the "stuff" that was wrong with
her. From the moment I moved toward her crib she let it be

known that she wanted to be picked up so badly that no scars, no bandages, no crew cut, nothing, would have stood in my way . . . or yours, had you been there. Lindsay Grice had won. I didn't even have a chance. She was that way with everyone.

I had been given permission—gladly by the busy nurses—to hold babies and give milk and cereal where medically approved, and even change diapers! Lindsay was my first diaper change in ten years. It must have given her a good laugh!

I have never received such rewards simply by holding a child. Her joy and contentment were almost pathetic. But then, the need had been acute: fifty operations in four years; lots of time in medical isolation, flat on her back, rarely able to be held . . . No wonder her need was acute.

We rocked and rocked and rocked. She played with my hair. She explored my watch. But mostly, she just held on . . . and smiled. And I unwound.

We must have sat that way for an hour. And I was planning to do so for hours more. I was on my "own time." I could do what I wanted.

"Chaplain, dial 4123." It was the speaker page, heard all over the hospital.

I wasn't on call that night; Al O'Connor was. He would have to answer. Craig Hatfield had been strict about that. "When the chaplain is paged, unless by name, only the person on call should answer," he had instructed.

"That's all right," I said to Lindsay. "I'm not on call tonight." She didn't care, of course, as long as I didn't move. But some parents in the room may have wondered. I had said it for their benefit, to get me "off the hook."

"Chaplain, dial 4123."

I got a bit uncomfortable. This time I didn't say anything. But I didn't answer the call, either. Craig had been very definite, I reminded myself. I didn't worry about the *reason* behind the call because I wouldn't let myself admit there was any possibility I'd answer it in the first place.

"Chaplain, dial 4123."

I put Lindsay down in her crib. She screamed. She had the right. I wanted to scream, too.

I went to the nurses' station. "May I use the phone?"

"Sure. It was 4123."

I didn't want to. I didn't want to hear the nurse say, "Please come to four-north right away." I didn't want to walk the L-shaped hall to the elevator and walk the L-shaped hall back to four-north, right above three-north. (Now I know there is a stairway that would have gotten me there in an eighth the time.) I didn't want to talk with the nursing supervisor in the starched white uniform with the starched white face.

I didn't want to. It wasn't fair. I wasn't on call.

A little girl, five years old, mongoloid, brought in for some tests, dropped dead while her parents were getting her undressed, the doctors don't know why, no idea . . . the nursing supervisor reported. "The parents are behind the curtain in the doctors' chart room, very upset, their names are Stone, Mr. and Mrs. James Stone, the little girl's name was Ethel."

She stopped. She waited. "Well, move!" said her eyes.

I moved. I didn't want to.

It was dark in the cubbyhole behind the curtain. There was a window. A street lamp cast a blue glow over the two huddled figures. The mother wore a purple wool pantsuit. Her hair was dyed black. The father, slightly balding, was holding a furry pink child's coat in his left arm. They were sitting on plexiglass chairs. And the only sound was of the plexiglass chairs . . . shaking.

"I'm a chaplain," I said. "Would you like to pray for Ethel?"

"Yes. Please . . ."

I've always wanted to thank those parents for what they gave me that moment. If it mattered that I was a woman, if it mattered that I was young, if it mattered that I didn't look like a chaplain, their faces didn't show it. There wasn't room for nitpicking, for stereotypes, I guess. In that moment of crisis I discovered that as long as a human being is there to offer support, to offer faith, she could have two heads. It wouldn't matter. And that fact never has changed.

"Dear God . . . We don't understand what has happened. It was so unexpected. We cannot comprehend . . .

"Dear God, please be with these parents now. Hold them up. Give them strength. Let them realize that there are some things in life that we, as human beings, can never understand. But that when these things happen we must rely upon your wisdom, dear God. For though we are told that your ways are not always our ways, we trust in your everlasting love for all of us.

"But one thing we do know amid the suffering in this room, dear God . . . We know, without doubt, that right now in this very moment you are holding little Ethel in your arms, next to your heart.

"Keep these parents there, too, dear God, in spirit. Renew their faith and let them understand that 'love never ends.' "

I don't know if it was a "good" prayer or not. I do know I didn't say it. Oh, the words came out, but I've never been sure from where. Though my mind tried to race ahead to form the thoughts, it didn't always get there in time. But the words kept coming out, one after another, in order. And that has happened more than once since.

I was awfully glad when it was over—the prayer. It happened too fast. My mind had barely left the aimless, drifting joy of holding Lindsay.

I had crouched down in front of the Stones to pray. It seemed closer that way. She had taken my hands. He had put his hand on my shoulder.

But after the prayer, I didn't know what to do next. I didn't have to know. The mother grabbed my arms, buried her head on my right shoulder, and sobbed. (Two hours later the patch of wool on my yellow sweater still was damp.)

I held onto her as best I could, crouched down in that dark

cubbyhole. The father put his hand on her shoulder. He was fighting back the tears. He was succeeding. But the rims of his eyes were like blood.

She said Ethel was their only child.

She said Ethel was their only child.

She said she couldn't believe it happened.

She said she couldn't believe it happened.

She said she couldn't believe it happened.

He said the doctors had only promised one year. They had had five . . .

She said she couldn't believe it happened.

"Excuse me . . ."

I hadn't heard her come in. It was a doctor in a light blue coat. Her red hair was tied back and she wore horn-rimmed glasses that kept slipping down on her nose.

"Excuse me. I wonder if you would agree to an autopsy?"

"Yes."

"We don't know yet what happened and that way we can determine whether it was the blood or the heart or the brain . . ."

"Yes."

"Thank you."

Uncomfortable. What to do? The doctor kept standing there. The mourning had been brought to an unnatural end.

So had the child.

The father got up. I got up. My knees hurt. The leg muscles pulled taut. Mascara had made a map of the mother's face. She fumbled for a Kleenex in a deep, junky brown purse. Someone, the doctor, opened the curtain wider. The light hurt.

"I'm sorry," said the doctor. She made a fumbling gesture to put her hand on the father's shoulder.

Too late, I thought. You interrupted. You blew it. Your timing was wrong. They weren't finished . . .

I wasn't finished. I haven't put it all together, inside me. Dammit. Doctors are supposed to be perfect.

A very young nurse handed the father a brown paper bag. A brown paper bag. She helped him stuff the size five furry pink coat into the brown paper bag that already contained a size five dress, shoes and socks and underthings. He nestled it in his arm, the brown paper bag, like a child. Only it wasn't.

I may never forget that.

I never saw Ethel Stone.

I went back to three-north. I needed Lindsay's rewards. I needed to hold a live child. I needed.

Lindsay stuffed me full of love. I was too limp, too drained to respond. But that didn't matter to Lindsay. All she needed was to be held. She did all the rest.

We rocked, I don't know how long. She fell asleep in my arms, I don't know how long. I didn't move.

Somehow, sometime, I got home. I wanted to go to sleep. But when I sat down on my bed something inside me clicked, like a grenade pin pulled. Nothing more could be put inside me before something was let out. There hadn't been time to sort, to digest . . . Not enough time.

I barely had the presence left to dial the telephone. I knew what was happening and I needed someone for it to happen on. There was only one person I trusted completely, trusted to understand: Dr. Davies, my minister, teacher, counselor, and friend for years. When he answered, it was like a button pushed, an explosion. A gusher of words and tears fell down all around me in piles on the furry bedspread.

I guess Dr. Davies understood the words. I know he understood their meaning. He gave me room to breathe and time to cry and showed the worth of silent presence.

I told about Tracy Marks.

I told about Ethel Stone.

I told about the brown paper bag. *The brown paper bag.*

"Why? Why?"

He got angry! At God.

At God? No, I was misinterpreting, I was too upset. It wasn't what I expected. It lashed out, his voice, at an unbound evil . . . and at God. At God? No.

Now I know. Now, one year and deaths and deaths later. Now I know. Now I begin to know.

But then? It wasn't what I expected. But he was there. He listened. He gave back. He was my friend, unfailing, as always.

I went to sleep, I guess.

The next afternoon I was waiting for an elevator at Children's. A doctor in a gray coat walked up with another doctor in a gray coat. The first man was the one who had been washing his hands, who had made the strange bow to me, who had given me the look when I returned to Bobby's room the first day—one week before!—it seemed like months.

"You're our chaplain," he asked in a statement.

"Yes . . . I'm assigned to three-north."

"I know. That's my floor. I'm Dr. Verdi, chairman of neurosurgery. This is my colleague, Dr. Praeder. You really ought to come on rounds with us. Do you like it?"

Pause. Whew!

"Yes, so far. I don't understand many of the medical terms, though."

"That's why you should join us on rounds. We're going right now. Come with us."

"All right." I figured I didn't have much choice.

Other doctors joined us on rounds. Some wore blue coats, some white jackets, some gray coats. I didn't know the difference. I didn't understand any of it. But I didn't faint.

I knew some of the parents, some of the children . . . like Gary Larson. How everybody loved Gary Larson! He was three. I had trouble looking at his head at first. But he didn't give up on me. He had hydrocephalus.

             Hydrocephalic babies are referred to by laymen as "waterhead" babies. I hate the term, but it's the best way to understand it, I guess.

We all have four cavities—cavities called ventricles—in our brain system: two lateral ventricles, left and right sides; a third ventricle; and a fourth ventricle. We also have a clear fluid, cerebrospinal fluid (CSF), that circulates within our spinal columns, ventricles, and brain.

When there is an increase in the amount of CSF, and an increase in the size and pressure in the ventricles, then a person may have hydrocephalus.

This increase in CSF and in intraventricular size and pressure —to try to explain the whole thing in lay language—can be caused by any of a number of different things: a congenital abnormality, an obstruction, a constriction, a birth defect called myelomeningocele (spinabifida), a tumor, a cyst . . .

If this hydrocephalus is not corrected, the baby's head can get bigger and bigger and bigger. And the baby can die.

To correct the effect of hydrocephalus—not cure it, unfortunately—a tube called a "shunt" is implanted inside the head into one of the ventricles. Then the tube, the "shunt" (which looks like a transparent, very thin, hollow string of spaghetti), is pulled just under the skin from the ventricle down the neck and, usually, into the stomach. And it stays that way. A tube, draining excess CSF from the ventricle into the stomach cavity, where it is absorbed naturally.

Sound grotesque? Have you ever seen a person with untreated hydrocephalus? Shunts are beautiful.

Gary Larson had a shunt. About twelve shunts in all while I was there. Sometimes shunts get blocked. Not usually that often. But when they do, they have to be unblocked, or replaced. That's an operation, each time.

Gary had the longest head I had ever seen. It just went back and back, emphasized by the fact that his head had been shaved for surgery. Usually, if you notice the head of a hydrocephalic child at all, it looks bigger in front, at the forehead. But not Gary. His looked like someone had stretched it backwards.

I looked away fast the first time I saw the back of Gary's head. He was cute, face on. Maybe that's why I looked away. I didn't want to admit the rest of his head.

"What's your name?" he had asked that first time.

"Nina."

He repeated, "What's your name?"

"Nina." But I wouldn't give. I wouldn't say, "What's *your* name?" or "Can you say 'Ni-na'?" I moved on, to another bed. Gary had looked a bit puzzled.

Gary was there that first night when we made rounds, sitting up in his crib in his blue bathrobe and blue slippers. I waited at the door, looking up at the ceiling light.

"Hi, Gary!"

"Hi, Dr. Verdi. Hi, Dr. Praeder. Hi, Dr. McMahan. Hi, Dr. Craig. Hi, Dr. Suter."

I stopped looking at the ceiling light.

"You missed one, Gary. Who's this?"

"Uh . . . what's your name?"

"That's Dr. Mills, Gary."

"Hi, Dr. Mills!"

"Will you remember?"

"Hi, Dr. Mills!"

"How do you feel, Gary?"

"Fine."

"Does your head hurt?"

"No."

"Good boy! See you tomorrow. Bye."

"Bye! . . . Hi, Dr. Mills!"

"That kid remembers everyone's name. Don't know how he does it. We must have tickled something with all those shunts!"

Gary Larson had shown me! Another lesson. The more I knew Gary the less I saw his head. That happens a lot on three-north.

Thursday afternoons we had a staff floor meeting: the two head nurses, two social workers, physical therapy, recreational therapy, occupational therapy, home nursing coordinator, chaplain, and various other drop-ins.

I liked the meetings. At first I felt like an observer. They soon kicked me into participating. It was better that way. That's what made the meetings work; that and having central problems familiar to all.

Ostensibly, the purpose of the meetings was to discuss the current status of each child on the floor, physically, emotionally, educationally, etc., and the status of his or her family. That's what happened, too—total care, not just words.

But more than that happened at those meetings. They reminded us that we weren't alone, that each of us was getting knocked down by our emotions every now and then, and that maybe it would hurt less when we talked about it in a group once a week. Two can hurt as cheaply as one? In the chaplain group the children were different and and the specialty was central; in this group the specialties were different and the child was central. I guess I just functioned better in the second type than the first.

It was right after such a meeting on Thursday afternoon that Mrs. Cooke asked me if I knew Mrs. Salvador.

"Yes, Jason's mother."

"Well, she's taking that baby home. She just gave me the discharge slip. She shouldn't, you know. He needs surgery. The doctors think he has hydrocephalus and needs a shunt . . . though it was a difficult diagnosis as I understand it. Anyway, I guess his mother is scared. She's leaving with Jason . . ."

"Do you want me to talk with her?"

"Please. But I don't know if it will make any difference now. Good luck."

"I'm leaving. I don't know what else to do. That doctor didn't make any sense. I came here for medical answers, and suddenly I have to make all the decisions. I can't decide something like that, so I'm leaving."

"What did the doctor say?"

"I don't believe it. I still don't believe it. But I know I heard him right. He said Jason *may* have hydrocephalus—*may* have. Now, he says he can operate and Jason will get better, or he can operate and Jason won't get better, or he can *not* operate and Jason will get better, or he can *not* operate and Jason won't get better. And he says my husband and I have to decide what to do! Can you beat that? *We* have to decide. He's the doctor!"

"Did he make a recommendation?"

"No, none. If he would have I probably would have gone along, either way. After all, this hospital is supposed to be the best. But no, he said he couldn't make a recommendation at all. *We* have to decide. Well, I can't and my husband can't and we're going home."

"Which doctor told you this?"

"Dr. Verdi."

"The one with gray hair?"

"Yeah, in a gray coat; that's him. Do you know him?"

"Yes, I think I do." He had seemed straightforward, if he was the same doctor who had asked me to go on rounds—I was still having trouble getting all the names together—and I was surprised he would tell a parent something like that. I had never heard of a doctor not being able to recommend a course of treatment.

"Would you talk with him? Maybe I didn't hear right after all. Maybe you'll understand something I didn't."

"I'll try. Will you wait until I see if I can find him now?"

"Yeah. OK."

I went back to the nursing station. "Does that gray-haired doctor, his name begins with a 'V' . . . ?"

"Dr. Verdi?"

"Yes. Does he have an office here?"

"Yes. On the ground level."

"How do I get there?"

"Take the elevator to 'G,' then turn right. It's the first door after the lab. It says 'neurosurgery' on the glass."

"Thanks."

"You're going to try to see him about Mrs. Salvador?"

"Yes." I didn't even think to question the ominous tone in her voice.

       I almost burst into the neurosurgery office. There was Dr. Verdi putting on his topcoat.

"I *have* to see you for a moment. It's important. Do you have time?"

"Well, I was just going downtown"—he assessed my face and manner—"but yes, I have a few minutes. Go into my office."

It was small, but well appointed: a large desk, two leather chairs, two walls of X-ray lights, a bath off to the side, books and shelves, small table with ashtray, leather beanbag chair.

"I tell my secretaries the only time they can sit in the beanbag chair is when they wear miniskirts."

I smiled, but chose another place to sit. "I just talked with Mrs. Salvador. She's leaving."

"Mrs. who?"

"Mrs. Salvador, Jason's mother."

"Oh, yes. I talked with her earlier."

"I know. That's why she's leaving."

"Oh."

"She says you told her you could operate on Jason and he would get better, you could operate on him and he wouldn't get better, or you could not operate on him and he would get better, or you could not operate on him and he wouldn't get better; and that she and her husband had to decide for or against surgery. Now, maybe she didn't hear you correctly . . ." (I would be diplomatic.)

"She heard exactly correctly. That's exactly what I said."

My tone was even. "How could you? How can they decide? You're the surgeon." (Those last words scared me for a moment. Maybe he wasn't a surgeon. Maybe he just represented the surgeon. I still didn't know much about the medical staff hierarchy even though I had gone on rounds a few nights.)

"Yes, I'm the surgeon. But Jason is their child. All I can do is give them the results of the tests. How long are you going to be here?"

"Until the end of March."

He was very calm, sitting back in his chair, smiling. He had swung the chair around so he faced me directly.

"Good. That's not nearly long enough, but you may as well learn something while you're here. And since you're on my floor, I suppose I'm your teacher.

"Mrs. Salvador—and you—both would have a right to be upset with me if I had held something back, not given all I could. It wouldn't have been fair and it wouldn't have been medically ethical. Unfortunately, Jason's case is a difficult one. With some children I know the diagnosis is hydrocephalus before we even take the tests, just by touching the head, just by looking. That comes from experience. We take the angiograms to be sure, to have proof in black and white, and to determine the type of hydrocephalus, etc. But many times the minute I see the child I know the diagnosis. I can recommend immediately to insert a shunt. Do you know what that is?"

"What Gary Larson has?"

"Right. And I know that ninety times out of a hundred surgery will have an immediate, positive effect.

"But with Jason Salvador it's different. He has, for want of a better term, what we call 'normal or low pressure' hydrocephalus. I can't diagnose that at a glance. So we took a lot of tests and we're still not sure. We've ruled out a cyst and a tumor and neurological damage, so we're left with this, with normal or low pressure hydrocephalus. And we *don't* know whether inserting a shunt will make any difference.

"There's obviously something wrong with the child. At this time—he's nearly ten months old—he's way behind in his milestones. He can't roll over or hold up his head. But I honestly can't recommend surgery as a 'cure' or a correction of the problem. Because I don't know if it *will* cure or correct the problem. Do you see?"

It was months later until I really understood medically what Dr. Verdi had said. But I got the gist of it.

"Yes, I think so. And I appreciate the problem. But still, as a doctor, isn't it your responsibility to recommend a form of treatment? How can the parents decide?"

"They *have* to . . . in this case. Jason's their child. I wish I could recommend treatment. I wish the decision was clear-cut. It isn't. And I can't assume the role of parent. Suppose I'm wrong?"

"Suppose they're wrong?"

"They're the parents. Their decision will be based on love, and on the knowledge that they'll be responsible for caring for the child no matter what. They *have* to make the ultimate decision.

"Now, mind you," he continued, "if the reverse were true, I'd fight like hell. In other words, if I were sure surgery was necessary, was the only way the child's life could be saved, or be meaningful, and the parents refused, I'd have them hauled into court before you could say your rosary. Oh, you're obviously not Catholic."

"Presbyterian."

"Too bad." He winked. "With a name like Verdi, I'm not Jewish. Anyway, there I'd *know* my decision, *know* my diagnosis, *know* the odds, *know* what was necessary. There would be an operation no matter what." (I was to see this happen several times.)

"I agree with that. But what about Jason?"

"His mommy and daddy *have* to decide."

"What would you do if Jason were *your* child?"

"That's not a fair question. You're a good debater, and obviously concerned about this—I wouldn't be here talking with you if I didn't see that in you—but it's still not a fair question."

"Thank you. Why not?"

"Because I have an obvious prejudice. I'm a neurosurgeon, so naturally I would want to apply my skill, that for which I've trained my whole life, to try to save my child. I'd be looking at it with a different prejudice, a different set of values than Jason's parents. Yes, I'd operate if Jason were my child. But I can't tell Jason's parents that because it would be a personal prejudice rather than a medical opinion. Do you see?"

"Yes, but what if you were to say to them exactly what you just said to me; explain it just that way?"

Pause.

"All right, you win. Yes, I suppose I could do that. But it wouldn't be a medical recommendation. They'll have to understand that. They'll still have to decide.

"I don't like this kind of case either, you know. They don't come that often, thank goodness. I like to be able to be definite. But if it's not this, it's something else, I guess.

"Parents of children with tumors want to know *before* surgery if the tumor is malignant, if we can get it all, if there will be damage. Once a terminal diagnosis is made, they want to know how long the child has, what type of decline, how much pain.

"They're all fair questions; it's just that usually they're unanswerable. We don't know. Sometimes we can guess pretty close from experience. But if we were to tell the parents, they usually couldn't take it all at once anyway. And if it proved different from our guess, they'd be angry with us. People can hear only so much at a time. So I only give them so much at a time in most cases.

"I told Mrs. Salvador *why* I couldn't give a recommendation for treatment. I explained about the difficulties in diagnosis, about the difficulties in recommending treatment for normal or low pressure hydrocephalus. But all she heard was what she repeated to you, and that's why she was confused. She just couldn't hear it all and comprehend it all at once. That's normal. I understand that. It's hard.

"Tell you what," he continued, "I'll have a chance to see Mrs. Salvador at 11:30 tomorrow morning—if she's still here. It's up to her. But if she is, I'll tell her what you want me to tell her, and explain the whole thing again. And you'll see, she still won't hear everything. OK?"

"Yes, thank you. And thanks for your time."

"That's OK, I'm just late for a speech I didn't want to give anyway."

He probably was, too.

Mrs. Salvador was thirty-three; her husband was forty-two. He was a quiet man with slightly graying hair and an earnest expression. He was Croatian and foreign-born. Mrs. Salvador was slender, taller by a few inches than her husband, and had short brown hair. Jason was a handsome baby with big blue eyes, dark brown hair and a happy smile. But he couldn't lift his head, couldn't roll over, couldn't do other things that normal nine-month-old babies do. He was small for nine months, too.

They had room 384, a private room at the other end of the hall from the nursing station. It was next to the small waiting room where parents—and the chaplain—could smoke. (I've since given it up!) I met a lot of parents that way, in that little waiting room, without all the formal introducing of "Hello, I'm your friendly neighborhood chaplain." I would just sit there, have coffee and a cigarette, and conversation would come naturally, uninhibited, even with the clerical collar.

Mr. and Mrs. Salvador both were sitting in the small waiting room when I returned.

"Did you see him?"

"Yes. He said if you're still here tomorrow morning, he'll see you at 11:30 in Jason's room. But it's up to you whether or not you stay."

"Did I hear him right?"

"Yes, as far as the part about operating. Yes, he said you heard him exactly right."

"But how *can* we decide?" asked Jason's father. "I am not a doctor. I am not trained in medicine. I am a worker in a factory. I do a good job. I make decent living. I wait many years to find just right woman and to have baby. I want a son very much. Jason, he is my son, my firstborn. I am very proud. And now this. I cannot sleep. I cannot eat. I cannot do my work with properness. My child, something is the matter with my child. I *cannot* decide. How can I decide?"

He was nearly in tears.

"Come," he got up, "we go into room. Do you see?" he asked, sitting in an orange vinyl chair. "How can I decide?"

"Did he say anything more?" asked Jason's mother. "Anything that would help?"

"I think so. But I don't want to speak for him. He'll have to explain the situation and his thinking to you himself. I wouldn't want to risk misinterpreting anything medical."

"But you think we should stay?"

"If it were me, I'd at least stay until tomorrow and talk with him again. I don't think one more day could hurt. But that's your decision."

"Yes, she is right," Mr. Salvador said to his wife. "We will stay one more day, and listen again. This time I will be here, too. It is very important. It is our son. Too important to take chances."

The baby was asleep. Mr. Salvador got up and walked over to the crib. "He look so normal to me. I not know about 'milestones' —what Jason should do by age nine months. No one tell us. We think he have the flu. Bring him to doctor. Doctor say 'something more,' say Jason not meet 'milestones.' Suddenly Jason in hospital with many tests. I don't know. I don't know. He look so normal, so beautiful to me. Jason . . . Jason . . ."

He folded his arms on the crib railing and buried his head. It wasn't my time to be there. I nodded to his wife and started to leave.

"We'll stay. Tell Dr. Verdi we'll see him tomorrow, please," she said quietly as I left.

I felt he already knew that.

The surgery went well. But it would take months to know if it had made any difference, if it had been the "right" decision . . .

(I saw Jason Salvador last week, about a year after his surgery. He's holding up his head and rolling over and sitting up and walking and talking and getting into the general mischief that all normal twenty-one-month-old babies get into. He's right up with his milestones.

(The decision was "right." The surgery worked. Or would Jason have been this way without the shunt? We'll never know. His parents will never care.)

7.

I hadn't learned how to read medical charts yet
—or even realized that I was allowed to read them without someone slapping my hands. And even if I could have read them, I
probably wouldn't have understood many of the diagnoses. But
maybe reading Pat Allen's chart would have answered at least one
question.

When I look back, I can't believe how naive I was. There she
lay, in a coma, her eyes rolled back, steam to help her breathe
more comfortably. And I didn't know what was wrong with her.

I'd try to talk with her . . . in a coma . . .

She was six.

One day I saw a lady sitting beside Pat's bed. I stopped at the
doorway. "Hello, I'm Nina Herrmann. I'm the chaplain on three-
north."

"Hello, I'm Karen Allen, Pat's mother. Want to come in?"

"All right."

Visiting Pat Allen was not an easy task. She was in isolation.
One had to put on a blue gown, a paper mask, and rubber gloves.
(The same thing you had to do anytime you went into Room 380,
the eight-bed Neurosurgery-Neurology Constant Care room next
to the nursing station.

(That used to get me on rounds. It would always be a race to
see whether the doctors could finish before I felt as if I were going
to faint, all wrapped up in the mask and gown and gloves. I never
actually fainted. But the close calls came out about fifty-fifty.)

Inside Pat Allen's room I sat on an orange vinyl stool. Pat's
mother was sitting on a daybed. It was a private room. Mrs. Allen
was rubbing the little girl's arm. Pat had a crew cut—hair growing

out from an earlier operation? With her name and her hair, it wasn't until her mother referred to Pat as "she" that I was sure she was a girl.

I said a few words to Pat. So did her mother, maybe to make me feel more comfortable. "We don't know whether she can hear us any more or not. Sometimes I think she can and sometimes I think she can't. But I try anyway, just in case."

I should have realized right then. But I didn't. It wasn't that the thought entered my mind and I chose to push it out, to not accept it. The thought simply did not enter my mind, period. Looking back, I can hardly believe that.

But that was all Mrs. Allen wanted to say about Pat's condition. "But anyway," she went on, "what denomination are you?"

We discussed that, and talked about her family, and then I discovered that her husband was from England. A few falls ago I had spent five days driving through the English countryside. That was it. We had common ground to lessen the tension, though she was very pleasant all along.

She and her husband had taken their children to the British Isles the previous summer for a month. But Pat had been too ill to go. She told about the trip, the sights, the beauty, meeting her husband's relatives, how the other children had missed Pat, what they would write to her on their postcards, what she would write back.

It was a good story. She was happy and sad—and alone—in telling it. There was no way I could have appreciated or even vicariously participated in all the family love that went into that story.

The student chaplain who had been there before me could have. He had known Pat. He had been there for the diagnosis, for the surgery. He had been there through it all.

And now they had a chaplain who didn't even realize that Pat Allen was dying.

Less than two weeks later, she did.

I finally found out she was going to in one of our Thursday afternoon staff floor meetings.

In previous meetings when they had come to Pat's name they had said, "Just the same; no change. Her parents are OK," and gone on. But this particular week there was a guest social worker. When they came to Pat's name during the meeting someone commented that Dr. Craig had said that morning on rounds that "we should close the door and open the window" in Pat's room. It was explained to the visiting social worker that opening the window and closing the door was a frustrated wish that the *terminal* child could catch pneumonia and die more quickly.

(It sounds heartless, perhaps. But no one who said it or understood it was heartless. They just could do nothing more to save Pat Allen. And to watch her lying there, helpless, day after day, made the strain and suffering of her parents—and of the staff— greater and greater. To talk of opening the window and closing the door was "caring" about Pat Allen . . . caring about the dignity that is life in the face of the depersonalization that was her dying.)

"Terminal child . . ." The words stuck. I ventured to interrupt. "You mean Pat is going to die?" Everyone looked at me in utter amazement. They had forgotten what it was like to be so new, so unschooled in anything medical.

"Yes. Didn't you know?" asked Mary Cooke. But I guess she could tell by my face that I hadn't known. She was kind: "I'm sorry, I should have told you. I just thought you knew."

"I should have, I guess," I said quietly. And they went on.

The duty nurse called in a staff social worker when Pat died the following Monday morning. I don't blame her. I would have too. The social worker, Mary Lannen, had known the family from the beginning, just like the student chaplain who had preceded me. But Mary was still there. The student chaplain wasn't.

The staff social worker could be there when it counted—from

beginning to end. But not the chaplain; a new one every three months, like a tube of toothpaste, a disposable lighter.

I would have called Mary Lannen too, had I been the duty nurse.

It was the first time I sensed—for a floor like three-north, at least—that there may be something wrong with the Children's chaplain program. Not everybody finds it convenient to get sick and die within premeasured three-month periods. Some take longer.

Which comes first, the student chaplain or the patient?

With Marilee Johnson I was there from beginning to end. It made a difference, to me anyway.

Marilee was in a crib in the far right corner of a four-bed room, 391. Katharine Hanley was in the adult bed in the near left corner of the same room. Marilee was three. Katharine was twelve. They were hospital friends. Both were beautiful little girls.

Marilee would sit in her crib eating potato chips—always, it seemed—and plead "walk, walk" to everyone who entered.

She was the first black child I had ever held in my life. I was twenty-nine. To say it didn't feel any different would not be quite true. The mere fact that I thought about it—realized it as I picked her up—made it different.

I hope it's a difference my children will never notice.

Marilee pulled my hair; she played with my watch; the difference disappeared. It has never returned.

I walked with Marilee seated in the crook of my arm for hours, literally. She stayed unusually still for a three-year-old, and carried on ladylike little conversations. She was the most dainty three-year-old I have ever seen. That seemed to be everyone's word to describe Marilee—"dainty."

There were pictures of animals on a farm in the corridor between three-north and three-south, the orthopedics unit. We would stop by the pictures each time we walked and she would pick out each animal, repeating its name with perfect enunciation and pointing with a delicately arched finger.

Then there was the water fountain . . . always. "Drink, drink." (Have you ever tried to hold a child in one hand and adjust a water fountain with the other so the child's mouth and the stream of water meet? Well, try it!)

It seemed like the doctors were never going to get all the tests on Marilee they needed. It was a combination of "just one more test," and "we had to postpone the test until tomorrow."

That's how I met Marilee's mother, that and a prayer.

I had begun to stay at Children's later and later in the evenings, even when I wasn't on call. One evening I decided to take Marilee for a walk. When I went into her room an older lady was standing by her crib. I had on my collar. I said "hi" to Marilee and introduced myself to the lady.

"Oh, you know Marilee?"

"Yes, we take walks every now and then. I hope that's all right?"

"Oh, yes. It's perfectly all right. Marilee love to walk. I'm Marilee's grandmother, Mrs. Harris. I'm so happy to meet you."

"Thank you. I'm glad to meet you, too. I haven't had the opportunity to meet Marilee's mother yet."

"She be here when she can. She work funny hours. But she be here. I do wish the doctor hurry up and decide what he gonna do to Marilee, though. This waitin' is hard. Would you say a prayer for Marilee?"

"Yes."

She cried during the prayer, the grandmother. Not out loud, just running tears. I felt strange. I don't know why. Maybe it was her profuse gratitude at the end. That still makes me feel strange, uncomfortable.

The next evening I met Marilee's mother. But it was nearly two weeks and a number of conversations later that Mrs. Johnson began to let down her defenses, to talk comfortably.

It had been easier to talk about Marilee. The little girl had headaches and would lose her balance while walking so often that she was afraid to try any more. "Walk" to Marilee meant "in your arms." The neurosurgeons had tried a number of tests, and now they were asking to do just one more. Mrs. Johnson had about had it.

But it might have been less tense if she hadn't been worried about something else—her marriage. Her husband was a successful merchandiser. For a long time she talked as if nothing was wrong, he was just "away on business." He was.

But they were getting a divorce, too.

That came out one day when I wasn't expecting it. The two of us were sitting talking in the little waiting room. No one else was there. Mrs. Johnson had just been told that Marilee's final test was being postponed until the next day. All of a sudden I heard the whole story.

"Now I have to do all this alone; make all the decisions myself. She is *his* child, too. His own flesh and blood. You'd think he'd care.

"But I've been alone before; I can be again. I'm not going to fall apart like a shrinking violet, no sir. If he doesn't give a damn that's his business. He'll have to live with it."

I didn't have to say anything. She wasn't asking for that. Just my ears. It had taken a long time even for that, I realized. She continued the story for fifteen minutes, at least.

The next afternoon she asked me to pray for Marilee before her test. It was the first time.

Surgery was scheduled for the next morning. The test had finally shown that Marilee had a cyst in the lower back of her head. Cyst means "likely not malignant"; means they should be able to get it all. But check the statistics on posterior fossa cysts.

I remember seeing Dr. Verdi drive by in his little red Maserati about eight the morning of Marilee's surgery as I was walking the one block from Children's to Adult. He honked and I waved. "He'll be operating on Marilee in the next hour or so," I thought to myself. "I wonder how he feels, knowing that."

I had already been up to the sixth floor surgery waiting room to talk with Marilee's mother and grandmother before surgery. I promised to return later. It was my first experience with major surgery.

Dr. Verdi was good to parents during surgery. He would send someone out once or twice to give a progress report. Things like "surgery has begun," "they've approached the lesion" (cyst, tumor—the foreign area), "they're closing." It's good. It makes the parents and friends feel a little less in the dark, a little less helpless.

But one of the reports can be frustrating if it's not explained: the report about "closing." That makes the parents think the child will be in the recovery room momentarily. "Closing" to the parent means scalp sutures; "closing" to the neurosurgeon means hours of backtracking away from the lesion, being just as cautious as when they approached it. "Closing" means "from the lesion" not "of the scalp" in neurosurgery. It's a matter of hours versus a matter of minutes. A parent who doesn't realize this thinks something major has gone wrong, thinks the child has died.

They told Mrs. Johnson they were "closing" on Marilee at one o'clock. It was nearly three before we saw a surgeon. I arrived at about one-thirty. I could draw an exact picture of the face of that waiting room clock today, especially the minute hand. It was the hard way to learn what "closing" means neurosurgically. It helped the next time around. Then I could explain to the parents. But it didn't help Marilee's mother, because I didn't know what was going on then either. I was silently afraid she might have died, too.

The surgeon told Mrs. Johnson that Marilee was all right. It had been "delicate surgery" and she would have to be watched closely. But she was all right.

It's different from the movies, watching someone in real life relax after a terrible pressure has been lifted. It's as if they're a crumpled piece of paper being smoothed out, slowly, carefully, completely. There is no sudden sigh of relief like on the silver screen. It's quiet, subtle, unshareable.

Marilee's mother was the first person I had seen go through it. Mrs. Harris was more vocal. "Praise the Lord! Hallelujah! Praise the Lord God Almighty! Thank you Jesus!" It was a different world. It was an education, watching Mrs. Harris. But it was just as genuine.

Mrs. Johnson wanted to go to the chapel. There's a pretty children's chapel at Children's Hospital. There are services there on Sunday. We went there, the three of us. I remember my prayer was too profuse in thanks, like Mrs. Harris had been to me after my first prayer for Marilee. Maybe God was "uncomfortable" too, especially since he knew what was coming.

Or maybe that's why I remember my prayer as being too profuse. Maybe I wouldn't have remembered it at all if Marilee hadn't gone back to surgery at four that afternoon. Something had gone wrong.

I was down on three-north having a cigarette and talking with some nurses in the little room behind the nursing station. I had just recently been brave enough to venture in there. No one kicked me out. It was a very small area for nurses and doctors to relax without leaving the floor.

Someone stuck his head in and asked if I had heard that they took Marilee Johnson back to surgery.

"No! Why?"

"Something went wrong, I guess."

I went up to the sixth floor waiting room. There were Marilee's mother and grandmother huddled in the orange vinyl chairs. "Something went wrong. Something went wrong. I knew it couldn't last. I knew it was too good to be true."

We prayed. It seemed more "the thing to do" than anything else. We were too stunned to believe what we were saying.

I sat there, from four-fifteen on. I didn't leave. I didn't even know for sure if they wanted me to stay. But I had to. I had become involved. I had a vested interest. How dare God let me say a prayer of such profuse "thanks" and then let this happen. It was embarrassing.

It was about six-thirty. I was sitting on an orange vinyl stool. Mrs. Johnson was sitting on a similar one opposite me, knee to knee. Her mother was on a chair to my right. Her mother looked up toward the doorway. She stood and put out her arms. I looked up. I didn't believe what I saw.

There stood a large, stately black woman in a long white and silver evening gown with long sleeves and a high neck. She was wearing a large medallion and silver cross and she had a tiara in her hair. (I looked for a wand with a star on the end.)

Mrs. Harris and the glittering lady embraced. We were introduced. The glittering lady was a minister. She joined us and said a prayer. I don't remember a word of it.

I had decided I should leave. The glittering lady obviously was a family minister, I reasoned. I don't know if my feelings were hurt or not. I don't think they had room to be yet.

I slid my stool back away from Marilee's mother in a move to make a gracious exit. But before I could get up I felt a hand on my knee. "Don't go," whispered Mrs. Johnson. "Please; she's very nice, but she's my mother's minister, not mine. Please stay."

I stayed. Things worked themselves out. The glittering lady minister was very nice, and very aware of the situation. She did her "thing" and I did mine. But I sure watched a lot! I had never seen anything like it.

The clock became the focal point again, as if it were responsible, as if it could do something, as if it were holding back. No one ate. No one drank coffee. Soon, no one said anything.

Mrs. Johnson would take walks in the hall, each time either asking me not to leave or to come along. But she didn't talk much, just paced.

About eight that evening all four of us had gathered near the surgery doors. It just couldn't be much longer. Marilee's mother was sure Marilee would be dead. I was afraid she was right.

A doctor came out, motioned Mrs. Johnson over. They talked briefly.

"She's alive! She's alive!" She turned to us. Tears were streaking her face. "She's alive!" She almost staggered toward us. Her mother and the glittering lady minister rushed toward her, embraced her.

But she broke away. She came toward me and collapsed on my shoulder and sobbed.

I'm still sorting all the thoughts and feelings that raced through me then. But I think in that indescribable moment I wanted my father to see how color doesn't matter; I wanted a young minister at my church to see how gender doesn't matter; I wanted someone to see how tradition doesn't matter.

And I wanted not to be thinking about any of those things.

But I was two people, one participating and one watching. It would be easier to admit only the first.

The doctors knew then that Marilee very likely was going to die. I don't think her mother did. I know I didn't. I didn't know the signs. I didn't know the language. I didn't know the connotation of "respirator" in this case.

When I walked into Intensive Care a few minutes later they were trying to keep Marilee off one—a respirator. As chaplain I was allowed to go into Intensive Care anytime. Parents were allowed in for fifteen minutes at the beginning of every other hour.

Doctors and nurses were surrounding Marilee's bed; the doctors still dressed in green surgery scrub suits and white surgery shoes. Their shoes were spattered with blood and brownish-red sterile wash.

Dr. Verdi was bending over Marilee's bed, talking to her as if no one else was there. "Come on, Marilee, honey. Come on little girl. You're not cooperating, Marilee. You have to cooperate. Come on, Marilee, honey. This isn't good. It isn't good at all."

He went on and on.

He had a different look on his face. One I had never seen, and was rarely to see again. I remembered his smile of twelve hours earlier. It was no more.

He didn't notice me for a long time. I squeezed into a corner trying to be out of the way. I was mesmerized.

"Chris [Dr. Verdi's first name was Christian], Chris, we're going to have to hook her up," said a doctor I didn't know. "I don't see any other way. But we may lose her in the process."

"I know. I hate to do it. Come on, Marilee, honey. Please cooperate, please honey."

People were doing things to Marilee all the while. I don't know what. But everyone was moving.

Dr. Verdi saw me. He shook his head. His eyes dropped to the floor. "It's bad, Nina, honey," he said. "You better do your thing."

He turned away slightly and put his arms on the cabinet ledge by the window and looked out. It seemed like a long time. Then he went back to Marilee's bed. They were hooking her to a respirator.

It was the sound of her breathing and the multicolored blood pressure cuff and her shaved head that I remember.

Her breathing was a small whining, gasping, moan—a sound I had not heard before, and haven't since. At first I thought she was crying. After the respirator was in place I realized it had been breathing.

For adults, gray blood pressure cuffs are used. But in Intensive Care at Children's they had multicolored blood pressure cuffs. Anything for cheer. They used it so often on Marilee, I guess, that they just left it there that evening. It reminded me that she was a three-year-old child and children like bright colored things. Except she didn't see it. Ever.

Her head was shaved. The operation had been in the back but

they had shaved her entire head. She didn't look like the little girl who said, "Walk, walk . . ."

I went downstairs to three-north. I'm sure I rocked a baby, but I don't remember which one.

I decided to take one last look at Marilee before I went home. I found Dr. Praeder in Intensive Care. "We have to operate again."

I hadn't known Dr. Praeder very well before then. He had been the one with Dr. Verdi the day I was first asked to go on rounds. Maxmillian Praeder spoke with an accent, sometimes very heavy, but understandable. He was shorter than Dr. Verdi, a bit younger, and had black wavy hair. He was an "attending" physician. So was Dr. Verdi; only Dr. Verdi was chief of the service.

(I finally was beginning to figure out those things. Attending physicians wore gray coats. In neurosurgery they were Dr. Verdi, Dr. Praeder, and Dr. Len Craig, who I barely knew. Then there were resident physicians. They wore blue coats. There were several of them. I didn't know any that well yet. And finally there were medical students. They wore short white jackets and changed faces every few weeks. I never knew any of them well.)

Dr. Praeder was soft-spoken, a bit the opposite of Dr. Verdi, who always exuded a commanding, assured aura.

"I thought you went home."

"I was going to. Another surgery tonight?"

"Yes, I am afraid so. There is some bleeding."

"Is she going to be all right?"

"We do not know that yet. We just do not know."

We walked out of Intensive Care and sat on a window ledge. I was to have some major conversations on various window ledges in that hospital. This was the first.

"How does it look to you?"

"I cannot predict. But you must not get so involved. It is bad. You must be concerned, but not involved."

"It's my job to get involved, where I'm asked."

"But that is not good. You cannot perform at your best when you are emotionally involved."

"But I don't have to perform. I have to care. That's being emotionally involved at times. I can't just skip in, never having seen the parents before, and pray, and walk out. Not if I have the option. That's like 'put in a quarter, get your weight and a prayer.' Our jobs are different."

"I do not think so. If I become emotionally involved it is bad. It hurts my work."

Slowly I wondered if it were me or himself he was trying harder to convince. "But you do, don't you?" I ventured.

"No, I cannot. It is not good. Look, it is not good for you, either. You are pale and tired and upset. I'll bet you did not eat dinner."

"No. Did you?"

Pause. "No."

"And now you're going back to surgery again, right?"

"Right."

"And it's all routine. No feelings. Just a lump of clay."

"This conversation is supposed to be about you."

I would think clearer thoughts about a physician's emotional involvement. And I would change my thinking on its importance several times. But that was the first time I had thought about it. Both Dr. Praeder and I were to remember this conversation later —in May and June. But then we didn't mention it.

I went home, making Dr. Praeder promise to call me when the surgery was over to let me know the results.

Marilee lived. For three more days. If you call being on a respirator living.

She died Saturday morning. I was there. It wasn't like it had been with Tracy Marks. I knew Marilee was dead. She looked dead.

I didn't see her die. Her mother did.

Mrs. Johnson had just talked with Dr. Verdi about a half hour earlier. He had painted a dark picture.

She went in to see Marilee.

I had come up the back way from three-north. It was late morning. Things were always quieter on Saturdays, no surgery but emergency and only morning rounds.

I ran into Dr. McMahan. He was Dr. Verdi's "best resident." Dr. Verdi had told me that. He hadn't told Dr. McMahan.

Patrick McMahan was in his early thirties, brown hair, medium build, Irish, married with five children—all the same size! He had merged professionalism with understanding in a way almost no other surgeon I have met has been able to do.

But I didn't know that yet. I only knew he was friendly, willing to talk and explain things to me.

I bumped into Dr. McMahan by the back elevator on the sixth floor. "Hi, Rev. Coming to see Marilee? She's not doing too well. I don't think she'll hang on much longer. We won't let her, anyway. It's hopeless."

"Really?" That was the first time any of the neurosurgeons had put it into words for me. Dr. McMahan always would.

"What do you mean you 'won't let her'?"

"We'll pull the plug on the respirator."

"You can do that?"

"Somebody has to. It's legal in this state. We're getting no brain waves. Her EEG is flat, has been for three days now. [I didn't yet know what an EEG was.] It's just putting her family through useless agony. She's dead now."

"But who pulls the plug?"

"I would; but others would, too. We have to agree. It's done at times. It's just not broadcast. It's the only human thing to do."

I didn't really disagree. But I didn't understand it all either. I was still digesting the fact—now fact—that Marilee *was* going to die, period, no more questions.

Dr. McMahan went down in the elevator. I walked toward Intensive Care. As I reached the door, Dr. McMahan was being paged on the speaker and Mrs. Johnson was coming out . . . sobbing . . . but without tears. A nurse was with her. The nurse looked like she could have kissed me.

"She's gone. My Marilee. She died. Right now. I was watching, and she died." She walked aimlessly. It was only a few feet to the waiting room door, but she walked there in circles. She couldn't seem to stop and just cry. She kept walking and walking and zigzagging across the hall toward the door.

"She's gone. She's gone."

Mrs. Harris and the glittering lady minister were in the waiting room. They came out, heard the news, and began to wail, literally.

But Mrs. Johnson still was not crying. She still seemed to be in a strange trance. Dr. McMahan came out and took her into a little conference room to explain what happened medically. (No plug was pulled.)

He left and called me in. We sat there. In semi-darkness in the windowless room. She talked about Marilee, the things she did, the things she said. What she looked like when she was born.

I'm not sure she knew I was there. It didn't matter.

Then we prayed. In the middle, she wept . . . finally. It was beginning to make me nervous, her not crying.

A nurse came in and said she could see Marilee now, if she wished.

"Come with me, please." Mrs. Johnson took my hand and pulled more than really said anything.

I didn't want to go. But I did.

All the machinery had been unhooked. A sheet covered the little girl up to her neck.

We stood there by the side of the crib. The sun was blazing in. The room was very white.

Tears were streaming down Mrs. Johnson's face. But she wasn't making a sound. The room was quiet.

She pulled down the sheet and touched her little naked daughter all over. She rubbed her chubby little legs, her little tummy and chest, her arms, her cheeks. She lifted her shoulders gently and looked at the wound in the back of her head. Then she covered her again up to the neck.

Would I pray?

It was short. I don't remember the words.

She didn't seem to be able to leave. I didn't either. Suddenly my mouth opened and words came out. "You know, right now she's seeing something we can only dream of. She's seeing God's face."

I don't know where the words came from. I hadn't planned to say them. I hadn't even had the thought, the mental picture, before. But it broke the spell. Her mother kissed her on the cheek.

"Would you like to kiss her?"

"Yes." I did. She was warm, still.

"She's all right now," said Marilee's mother. "I know she's all right now. We can leave. God has her now. She's all right. My little girl's all right."

We left.

The last thing I heard Mrs. Johnson do before I took them to "admitting" to sign the papers was call her husband. He was in California, I think.

He wasn't in. For the last five days she had been trying to get him to come home to see Marilee. "You tell him his daughter . . . you tell him Marilee . . . she died. *She is dead.* You tell him that. You tell him to call me if he wants to know when the services are. If he gives a damn."

I realized I couldn't unwind yet when I walked back to three-north and saw Katharine Hanley. Someone had to tell the pretty little twelve-year-old about her former roommate . . . about Marilee, her friend. And someone had to deal with her reactions. It was only fair.

Her mother, that was the first place to start.

"How's Marilee?" asked Katharine's mother as I stopped her in the hall outside Katharine's room. Katharine was watching television.

"That's what I want to talk with you about."

"She died?"

"Yes."

"I was afraid of that when she didn't come back to her room for so long . . . But I don't think Katharine suspects."

"Do you want to tell her or would you like me to?"

"No, I'll tell her. But I know Katharine. She won't break down in front of me. She'll try to be brave. So, if you could sort of go back and talk with her after I leave, about eight tonight, I know it would help. I think she'll get it out with you, where I know she won't with me."

"All right. I'll talk with her later. I won't forget." What could I say? That I had a date at eight o'clock and I really wanted to go because I wanted to think about something else and be with somebody else, somebody who would yell at me enough to remind me I'm alive, like David. Oh well, he'd yell anyway when I asked him to pick me up here, at nine. Good old David.

Katharine's mother was right. I found Katharine, the curtains half-drawn around her bed, her eyes pointed at the television, with big tears half in and half out . . . with no safe place to cry.

"Wanna take a walk?"

She understood. "Yeah."

She put on her furry blue slippers and her striped housecoat. We found an unused private room, closed the door, put on only the night light, and she cried—it had been pent up for hours—all over my shoulder and the daybed. Just went limp and cried. It almost scared me how hard.

She didn't talk for a long while. Neither did I. There aren't any rules for times like that, no pat set of answers, no pat set of actions. You just wait, and hope you can avoid saying the wrong thing, whatever that is.

"Did she have any pain? I mean a lot of pain?"

"No. None at all. She just fell asleep."

"Good. I'm glad. I'm glad she didn't have any pain."

Pause.

"I used to carry her around, and give her potato chips, and push her in the wheelchair, and talk to her when she cried. She was so cute. She was so happy. She'd say, 'walk, walk . . .' I kissed her good-bye before she went to surgery. She said, 'bye, bye.' Oh, I loved her so much."

She cried again, all over again, the same way, just as long.

"I loved her so much. Why? Why did she have to die? Why?"

Pause. She wanted an answer.

"No one knows why people we love have to die. Only God knows that. And he loves us. So he must always let happen what's best for us in the long run. Marilee was a sick little girl. Maybe God knew if she lived she'd have a lot of pain, that she'd never be well and happy. So maybe he let her die and come to him in heaven so she wouldn't have to suffer, to have unbearable pain. You and I wouldn't have wanted her to have lots of pain all her life, would we?"

"No."

"Well, maybe that's what would have happened. I don't know. But I do believe God knows best and, in the end, always lets only those things happen to us that are best for us, even if we don't always understand at the time."

She thought. "Yeah. I wouldn't have wanted her to have lots of pain. And I remember she did say, 'head hurt, head hurt' lots of times."

Pause.

"Is she in heaven now?"

"Yes."

"Will I get to see her when I go there?"

"Yes."

"Will she recognize me? I'll probably be old."

"Do you believe that in heaven God can do anything?"

"Sure."

"Then don't you think he'll make it possible for two people who love each other to know each other again in heaven?"

"Yeah, sure! I guess he can."

Pause.

"I won't forget her. I'll never forget her. I loved her. I wish she wouldn't have died. But if she's happier in heaven and doesn't have any pain, I guess that's better. Is her mom OK?"

"Yes, I think so."

"Did you tell her about heaven and no pain?"

"In a way. But I think she understood. Mommies have a way of understanding. They always want what's best for their children, just like God."

"Yeah, my mom says that to me, sort of. I mean about wanting what's best for me. Can we sit here a little longer?"

"Sure. Do you want to say a prayer for Marilee?"

"OK, that would be nice." She took the "you" to be a personal you. I was glad.

"Dear God . . . Please take care of Marilee. I loved her so much. I really miss her. But I'm glad she's not having any more pain. I'm glad she's with you if she couldn't be happy here. But I miss her. I'll never forget her. I hope her mom's OK. Amen."

She sat very quietly. She got up and looked out the window. Beyond the street lamp. "See the star up there. Maybe that's Marilee."

"Maybe."

"My grandpa's in heaven. Now I know two people in heaven . . . and God . . . and Jesus . . ."

The Sunday after Marilee died I had the chapel services at both Adult and Children's. At Adult I decided to preach about God's love. I was going to steal a bit of Dr. Davies' theology about God's "unconditional love." It's a sound theology, I believe it, and maybe I needed to hear it that Sunday.

It was my first sermon.

(Here I must point out something, in retrospect. I wasn't wrestling with deep theological questions those first few weeks as a hospital chaplain, especially the theological questions related to pain and suffering and death and dying. I was simply flying by the seat of my faith, lots of times not sure where the next words or the next portions of gut strength were going to come from. When I went home at night I didn't always sleep. And when I did lie awake, the only things that went through my mind were the picture slides of memory. The people—the children—would flash over and over again in front of my eyes. *What* had happened to the people—the children—would flash over and over again in front of my eyes. But that was all. My head was full. There was no room for the "why?" Just no room.)

But back to God's "unconditional love" and my first sermon.

The services at Adult were held in an all-purpose chapel-conference room. Leftover styrofoam cups sat with dead cigarettes in musty ashtrays, and chairs had to be put aside to make room for the fifteen or so wheelchairs. Somehow I felt like I was preaching at a drive-in movie. The patients probably felt the same way.

"Most of you likely have heard God defined as 'love.' It's on bumper-stickers and buttons—and that alone should prove its validity! And it's also in the Bible: 'He that loveth not knoweth not God; for God is love.' [I John 4:8, KJV] And, as the verse says in the beginning, by loving we can know God—know his personality: 'He that loveth not knoweth not God.' Or, conversely, using preacher's license: He that loveth knoweth God; 'for God is love.'

"Now, let's test that, let's see what comparisons we can draw between God and love as we know it. And I'm not talking about people who use the word 'love' to get what they want. I'm talking about the most genuine forms of love that you and I have ever felt. And even these cannot come close to God's love."

"Amen!" stated an older black lady near the front.

A bit surprised, I smiled with her and went on. But my mind flashed back for a second to the black student in my preaching class at divinity school. "You whites miss all the *fun* of preaching," he had said. "We have help, support, from our congregations. It's real community!" I kind of knew now what he had meant. At least I knew someone was listening, was following.

"I assume most of us have experienced love in our lives: love for parents, brothers, sisters, friends, man, woman, wife, husband, grandparents, grandchildren . . . There are many kinds of love.

"But let's ask some questions about love. Can we see love? Can we touch love, literally? Can we buy love? Can we earn love by racking up points? Can we bargain for love? Can we turn love on and off like a light switch? Can we have control over love? Does love know the boundaries of race, creed, age, sex, nationality, wealth, social position?"

The lady had been shaking her head "no" with each question. So had—with less vigor—one or two others in the group.

" 'No' to all so far?" I asked.

"That's right!" said the lady.

"Can we reject love? Yes. Yes, we can reject love. But by rejecting love does that always stop the other person from loving us?

"Is love better when it is given with no demands, no strings attached? Is love better when it is there on our bad days as well as our good days? Is love better when it supports us, when it affirms us as persons, when it makes us feel totally safe and totally free at the same time? Some 'yeses' now?"

"That's right!"

"And, finally, is this love best of all when it is *all of these things* —all of these 'yeses'—and when we *respond* to it? When we feel the same way? When we try to love the other person the same way back? Another yes?"

"Amen!"

"Have you figured out my ploy yet?"

The lady nodded and smiled a huge smile. I smiled a huge smile back. Good for her! I sensed others were with me, too. It felt good.

"Let's look at God now, as we see him—or as I see him, anyway —and ask the same questions.

"Can we see God? Can we touch God? Can we manufacture God? Can we buy God? Can we earn God by racking up points? Can we bargain for God? Can we turn God on and off like a light switch? Can we exert control over God? Does God know the boundaries of race, creed, age, sex, nationality, wealth, or social position?

" 'No' so far? Are you seeing the parallels between love and God as we know them?"

"Amen!"

"Can we reject God? Yes. But by our rejecting God does he cease to exist? And does his love for us stop?"

"No sister, no!"

"Does God come to us with no demands, no strings? Maybe we're not too sure about that one, even if we've answered 'yes.' *Does* God come to us with no demands, no strings?

"Is he there on our bad days as well as on our good days? Does God support us, affirm us, as persons? Does he make us feel totally safe and totally free at the same time? 'Yes' so far now?"

"Yes!"

"And, finally, is God 'best of all'—do we feel him closest of all —when we *respond* to his love? When we try to love him back? 'He that loveth not knoweth not God; for God is love.' "

"Amen!"

"Now, if you think there are some variables in some of these last questions . . . then your *pride* is getting in the way. Yes, your pride . . . and my pride!

"What do I mean? Well, *were* you wondering whether God really makes no demands on us? Whether he really puts no per-formance strings on his love for us? Whether he really makes us feel totally free?

"Yes. The answer still is 'yes.' God loves us—each one of us —no matter what we have done, what we are doing, or what we will do. He loves each one of us equally, and totally without condition. Nothing, *nothing* you or I can do will make God stop loving us. Nothing."

"Tell it!"

"That is 'unconditional love.' And that is what makes God's love for us perfect and our love for each other, and for God, imperfect.

"For we, you and I, can't love without condition. We can *try* to love without condition. But sooner or later, from time to time, our pride gets in the way.

"Someone we love will hurt us and we'll say, 'You can't do that to me!' Someone we love will ignore us, will do something of which we don't approve, not live up to our expectations, what-ever. And sooner or later, we'll be too proud—whether it's hurt pride or snobbish pride—we'll be too proud to go on loving them. Our love will have been based on a condition."

"That's right!"

"And we do it to God, too. When all goes well, that's fine. But let us ask for something we don't receive, ask fervently and for a long, long time . . . And finally, when we don't get whatever it is we're asking for, our pride is hurt. 'I've lost my faith,' we sigh."

Softly, "That's right."

"So, strange as it may sound, if you—and I—think God doesn't love us because we've done too many things wrong, or because we've ignored him too long, or because we've simply rejected him, or because our prayers haven't been answered the way we want —it's just our pride getting in the way.

"Just because you and I can't love without condition doesn't mean God can't love without condition. And that's *our* problem —yours and mine, not God's.

"For God is totally *prideless.* That means he's totally humble. He'll love us always, without condition. He'll love us when we love him back and he'll love us when we ignore him—whether we ignore him because we think we've done too many wrong things, or because we don't have time, or because we are afraid we don't believe any more, or because we've 'lost' our faith . . . or because we've *never* believed. It doesn't make any difference. God will love us. Period."

"Amen!"

I smiled and lowered my voice just a bit. "But, in our lives when we have had rare moments of loving and being loved by someone who seems to love us without condition, someone who loves us in the midst of our stumblings, in the midst of our sufferings, how does that make us feel? Free? Not worried about always doing the right thing or saying the right thing? Safe? Secure that the love will not fly away on a whim?"

"That's right."

"And when we feel both free in love and safe in love, what does that do to our lives?

"It makes them other people directed, doesn't it? Suddenly we're not so worried about me, me, me: 'Nobody loves *me*, nobody cares about *me*, nobody listens to *me*.' Suddenly, the 'me' is loved and cared about and listened to, so the 'me' is safe, and free—free to see the world around him, free to see the world around her, and the people in it. Free to care for and love and listen to . . . somebody else."

"You said it! Amen!"

"And it's the same with God's love. When we *respond* to God's love—something that has been, is, and will be ours, freely, for all time no matter what—when we respond to God's love, suddenly we are safe, and we are free. We are safe in the knowledge that God loves us, God cares about us and God listens to us—unendingly; and therefore, we are free, free to see the world around us and the people in it. Free to care for and love and listen to . . . somebody else.

"Simple, isn't it? Almost too simple, too good to be true. And that's why we continue to try to build a self-righteous fortress around God, to make him someone *we* have to 'find' through good deeds and righteous feelings, rather than someone who *has already found us, where we are, today;* someone who loves us without condition and asks only that we accept that love and respond to that love.

"God *is* love, unconditional love. And knowing that and responding to that can make all the difference . . ."

"Praise the Lord and Amen!"

I was glad for the lady in the congregation. Not only did I know that at least one person was following, but I sensed that she helped others follow, too—or at least stay awake!

But I was also glad the sermon was over. I believe in God's unconditional love. It has made a major difference in my life. And it certainly has set me free. But that was the first time I had tried to put Dr. Davies' theology into a sermon, into my words. I was glad he wasn't there!

The people did seem to like it, though, afterwards. But I guess ministers never can tell for sure. I mean, very few people would go up to a minister and say, "That was a crummy sermon and it took too long and you speak in a monotone." They just say that to their spouses over brunch.

Anyway, I packed up my Bible and headed the one block west to Children's for the service there. This one would be easier, maybe. But what if a child got sick or a parent got really upset?

It was going to be difficult to strike a happy medium of speaking both to parents and children.

There were fifteen children and ten adults at the service. I hadn't expected that many. My knees got weak, very weak. I had written a few notes, but I just put them aside and decided to wing it.

Gary Larson was there. Remember Gary, who knew everybody's name? And Lindsay Grice, the little girl I rocked so often that first week. Gary and Lindsay were side by side in their wheelchairs. And they were the only people in the whole chapel I knew!

First of all we sang a hymn and then we went around the circle of parents and children introducing ourselves. At least half the children were in wheelchairs or "banana" carts and had I.V. fluid bottles attached to their arms. There were bandages on heads, chests, arms, legs, backs . . . everywhere.

But the smiling and the chattering and the bashful glances, they were the same. Children are children are children, I guess.

We talked about praying, about talking with God, and that there are many reasons to talk with God, and that it doesn't have to be a particular time or a particular place or a particular way.

Sometimes we talk with God when we sing, like the hymn. Sometimes we talk with God about happy things. Sometimes we talk with God about sad things. Sometimes we ask God to help us. Sometimes we thank God for helping us.

"And sometimes we think God isn't listening to us . . . don't we?

"But does God stop listening to us? Or does he sometimes know what's best for us even when we might not agree or understand?

"For example: do your parents really want you to be in the hospital? Of course not. But is being here the best way to help you feel better?

"Do the nurses really want to hurt you when they give you a

shot?" Laughter. "No, believe it or not, they don't. But is the shot to help you feel better?

"It's the same way with God. He doesn't like to see us un-happy, to see us hurt, but he knows many more things than we do . . . even many more things than our mommies and daddies and all the big doctors and all the nurses . . . and the chaplain! He knows, when all is said and done, what is best for us.

"And most important of all, God loves us. So in the long run, he'll only let what's best for us happen, even if we or our mom-mies and daddies can't seem to understand that right now, and even if we or our mommies and daddies get angry.

"We all do, sometimes, get angry because we don't understand what's happening to us and to those we love.

"But that's where faith comes in. God told us he loves us, and we have to believe he does—or go it alone. The choice is ours. Just like we really know our parents love us even when we don't always understand what's happening to us or why they tell us 'no' sometimes. Right?

"But it makes it better, doesn't it, when we talk with our parents about how we feel?

"And that's the same way with God. It's better when we tell him what we feel—when we're happy, when we're sad, when we're angry, when we don't understand. Because God is *always* listening. He always cares. And he'll always do what's best for us in the long run, because he loves us.

"And we'll also feel better about it if we talk with God. It will make us feel safer and stronger and braver. Because he'll be *sharing* our feelings with us!

"So that's what we're going to do this morning. We're going to talk with God. Each one of us will have a chance to say exactly what he or she feels . . . and we know God will be listening."

A little girl with her arm in a cast, suspended from a pole, went first: "Thank you God that I had a good operation and my arm will soon be better."

The others followed, happily without much prodding.

"Thank you God for my puppy. His name is Sam. I love him very much. He's a beagle."

"Please let me go home soon, God. And please help Mommy not to cry so much."

"Thank you for my grandpa. I wish I could see him. Please help him get well."

"Please let them let my sister come to visit me. I miss her."

Then we came to Gary Larson.

"Hi, Nina!"

"Hi, Gary!"

"Hi, Nina!"

"Gary, what do you want to say to God today?"

"What do I want to say to God today." It was a statement.

"Can you think of anything? God's right here with us. Don't you want to say something to him?"

"What do I want to say to God today." Statement.

"Can you say, 'Thank you, God'?"

"Yep."

Pause.

At the top of his lungs, "Thank you God!"

"Good, Gary! And this is Lindsay next to Gary . . ."

"That's Lindsay Grice!" clarified Gary.

"That's right, Gary. Lindsay, can you say, 'I love you God'?"

"Lindsay . . . say 'I love you God,' " Gary nudged her.

Lindsay mouthed the words, sort of. And smiled a huge smile.

"Good, Lindsay!"

And we went on . . . to some parents.

"I guess we don't understand all the time, God. Please give us courage. And help us turn to you more often. We've found comfort today. Thank you, God."

"Dear God, help us accept . . ." The rest was cut off by a choke.

"Dear God, thank you that we're taking our Tommy home with us next week. Help us remember what we have learned in this hospital. It has been a priceless lesson."

Back to the children.

"Thank you God for my turtle. His name is Harvey."

All this time Gary Larson had been looking all around the room, at the ceiling, the floor, the altar, the walls, the doorway.

"Hey, Nina!" Right in the middle of the prayers.

"Excuse me. Yes, Gary?" He was too little to understand.

"Hey, Nina!"

"Yes, Gary, what is it?"

"Where *is* God?"

It broke the growing tension. The little boy had been looking high and low for God in the chapel!

"That's a good question, Gary." And a hard one! "God is here, but he's inside us. He helps us feel happy. Do you feel happy now, Gary?"

"Yes!"

"Well, God helps us feel happy. OK?"

"OK. Hi, God!" He looked at his tummy.

Whew! I thought, and looked up as one of the fathers was smiling and making a gesture of wiping his brow. At least I got some sympathy!

We finished prayers. We sang a hymn.

"May the road rise to meet you. May the wind be always at your back. May the sun shine warm upon your face, and the rains fall soft upon your fields. And, until we meet again, may God hold you in the palm of his hand."

It was over. But the service and that Gaelic blessing—later requested by parents whose dying child I never saw, never was on my floor—had so affected those parents that I received two letters and a Christmas card from them long after I left Children's. Here is part of one letter. You never know, I guess.

> We will long remember the Sunday worship service you conducted in the hospital chapel the day we first heard the words of the "Irish Blessing." That was a most memorable half hour for us. It was perfectly done and so reassuring to us.
>
> Every weekend Bill was in the hospital we attended those

services, and for us, the Sunday you were in charge proved to be the most meaningful. You gave us a great deal of strength, and we want you to know that your ministry at Children's is much appreciated.

Having Bill gone leaves a huge void in our lives and a deep hurt in the pit of our stomachs. But we do have peace knowing that he is God's child and that he is with Him, suffering no more.

God bless you in your work.

You're right it made me feel good . . . and lots of other things.

The first time I saw Riann (pronounced: Ryan) Miles she was in room 383 sitting up in bed reading. It was early afternoon. Her hair was thick and dark, and about three-fourths of an inch long all over her head. If she hadn't been so pretty, she would have looked like a rosy-cheeked eight-year-old choir boy.

"Hi."

"Hi."

"What's your name?"

"Riann Miles—R-I-A-N-N, I'm a girl."

I smiled. "I can tell! I'm Nina Herrmann. I'm the chaplain on this floor. Did you just come in?"

"About an hour ago. My mother went downstairs for a cup of coffee. I didn't know they had lady ministers?"

"There aren't too many of us. I hope you don't mind?"

"Oh, no! I think it's a nice idea."

"What grade are you in?"

"Second."

"Where do you live?"

"Rock Shores."

"I like that town. It's pretty."

"Thank you, I like it too."

She was very polite, and very sweet, and very pretty. "Have you been here before?"

"Yes, three times: last August, then in October, and then at Christmas."

"Oh, Christmas; that's too bad."

"Oh, no, I was lucky. I got to go home just before!"

"That's good. I have to go to a meeting now. But may I come back to see you again?"

"Yes, I'd like that. I want my mommy to meet you."

"Thank you, I'd like to meet her, too."

       I met Riann's mother and her father that evening on rounds. Dr. Verdi introduced us, mentioning that they, like him, were Roman Catholic . . . teasingly implying that that was obviously a step above Presbyterian. Dr. Verdi clearly liked the Mileses and Riann. It was more like a social visit between them than a medical one, or at least those were the overtones.

Dr. Verdi pushed on Riann's stomach a few times. One place hurt. Did her head hurt?

"Just a little, not much."

"A headache?"

"Yes."

"When?"

"In the mornings, mostly."

Dr. Verdi told Riann's parents he hoped it was her shunt rather than anything else. He wanted to get her through her adolescent developmental stages before he had to do anything more major . . .

They nodded in agreement.

I wondered if she had something wrong with her stomach . . . But a shunt? She didn't look like she had hydrocephalus.

About an hour later I saw Dr. McMahan in the room behind the nursing station. "Do you know Riann Miles?"

"Yeah, cute kid. Did you meet her?"

"Yes, this afternoon and again near the end of rounds."

"Didn't make rounds. What did Verdi say about her?"

"He pushed on her stomach and asked her about headaches and said he hoped it was her shunt."

"Yeah, me too. I'd be afraid to go in there again, afraid of what I'd find."

"Does she have hydrocephalus?"

"Oh—you mean because of the shunt. Yeah, in a way. She's got two shunts."

"Two? Why?"

" 'Cause she has a big, nasty, ugly tumor in her head."

Pause.

He continued. "She's a beautiful little kid with a very ugly tumor." He looked at my face. "I'm sorry. Didn't you know?"

"No. What does it mean?" I felt sick.

"We don't know for sure."

"Is it malignant?"

"No, not by itself. But it acts malignant because we can't get it all out and because it may grow. Sometimes tumors like Riann has grow slowly, very slowly. That's what we're hoping. Verdi thinks she can have fifteen to twenty years. But I'm never as optimistic as he is."

"What do you think?"

"I don't know. But I just don't think it will be fifteen to twenty years . . ."

"Why does she have two shunts if she has a tumor?"

"Because the tumor puts pressure on the intraventricular system and can obstruct the flow of CSF. And by putting in shunts, we can relieve the pressure. They—the shunts—keep the person from getting bad headaches and having lots of pain. That's why we think that one of her shunts is either loose or obstructed now, because she has headaches."

"Obstructed by the tumor?"

"No, not likely. Just by some foreign matter caught in the end, maybe the tummy end. That's why Verdi pushed on her tummy."

"And if it isn't the shunts . . . if they aren't clogged, obstructed?"

"It may be her tumor . . . growing. That's why Verdi wants it to be the shunts. Not very pleasant is it, Rev?"

"No."

"But don't worry too much. I really do think it's one of the shunts this time. We'll know Monday after we do some tests. We're just going to observe her over the weekend."

Pause. "Did Pat Allen have a tumor?"

"Yeah, but a different kind. Other than shunts, we couldn't even operate on hers . . . it grew so fast."

"But it was a tumor?"

"Yeah, it was a tumor."

Saturday rounds are brief, around noon. Paul was going to pick me up at one o'clock for lunch and some shopping. Paul was just the opposite of David—sympathetic, easily moved, upset by suffering and illness. Visiting three-north, David would have calculated the amount of money spent on the surgical gauze used to cover wounds. Paul would have calculated the amount of suffering spent on the wounds that were covered by the gauze. But maybe I'm being a little hard on David.

Knowing Paul, I told him to go to the Information Desk when he arrived and ask them to telephone me on three-north and

I would meet him in the lobby. Paul wasn't ready for three-north.

But all Paul got out of his mouth was "three-north" and he was told to "go right up," and given detailed instructions on how to get there. (Paul was a public official whose face was well known.)

I was on rounds with the neurosurgeons, at the very farthest end of the L-shaped three-north wing. To get to me, Paul had to walk through about one-third of the orthopedic section, past all the private rooms on three-north, past the Constant Care room on three-north, and past all the four-bed wards on three-north. He had to walk past children with bandages and tubes and no hair and scars and casts and open backs and all those ailments I saw on my first day on three-north. He had to walk by all that. And he had to remember to smile pleasantly . . .

I was standing at the doorway of room 388, the last room in the hall. I felt a tug at my sleeve. I looked down; a child tugs at your sleeve. I saw a pair of highly polished boots and custom-tailored trousers: Paul. I looked up. His face was so white it was almost translucent. Poor dear. He looked so pathetic that I almost wanted to laugh.

"Oh, hi. We're just finishing rounds. Want to come along?"

His head shook no.

"Want to wait on that chair? I'll only be a few minutes. I promised to see one little girl for a minute before I leave."

His head shook no.

"Want to wait in the lobby?"

His head shook yes.

"Can you find your way back to the elevators?"

His head shook no.

"OK, I'll show you."

His head shook yes.

I walked with him back to the elevator. He never said a word. He had that stupid, plastic-politician smile on his face. But behind it was silent panic. When we reached the elevator he kissed me, got in, and went to the lobby . . . or so I thought.

But when I got to the lobby, Paul was gone. I looked downstairs, and in the emergency waiting room; even in the chapel. Nowhere. So I decided to wait. After all, I couldn't look in the men's room.

Five minutes later he came in the front door.

"Sorry. You been waiting long?"

"No. Where did you go?"

"Come on, I'll show you."

We got to his green Continental and the right front seat was littered with scraps of paper. The door to his glove compartment was open and everything inside was arranged in neat piles.

"I was so frustrated by what I saw that I couldn't sit still. I cleaned out my whole glove compartment, found things I never knew I had, tried to forget. I couldn't."

And all through lunch he couldn't forget.

He still hasn't.

He never went back.

I knew he wouldn't.

They operated on Riann Miles Monday afternoon. It was her left shunt, blocked, at the top end—in her ventricle.

Dr. Verdi was optimistic. Just her shunt he told her parents. She can go home in about ten days.

But Dr. Praeder had done the surgery. "I think the tumor, it is growing. I do not know for sure. But I think it is bigger than before. I think we must watch very carefully." He was saying that to Dr. McMahan after rounds Monday evening. I overheard.

I remembered Pat Allen.

One evening Riann and I were playing the card game "war." I could see that she was getting tired. I was glad in a way. I hate "war."

"Wanna just talk?"

"Yes, I think so. Thank you."

That was another unusual thing about Riann, beyond her unswerving politeness. Winning was of no importance. Neither was finishing a game. What eight-year-old do you know who would have stopped in the middle of a card game—tired or not—without saying, "OK, but I win"; or, "OK, but we have to draw to see who wins." I don't know any, except Riann Miles.

"We say prayers at home in my room."

"You mean the whole family?"

"Yes. Or, at least Eric and Kevin and Allison and Mommy and me, if Daddy isn't home. We have relics, crosses and things my grandmother gave us. We use those in our prayers."

She started to giggle. "You know what my brother Kevin did? —he's so funny. The last time I was here I asked him to bring some of the relics so Mommy and I could say prayers here. And he brought them in—you'll never believe this—in a Seagram's bag!" Giggle. Giggle.

"In a what?"

"A Seagram's bag. You know, like liquor comes in. It was really funny."

"Oh," I laughed with her. "That is funny." I still wasn't quite sure what she meant, but I guessed she meant her brother had put the crosses in a blue velvet Seagram's Crown Royal bag. (I was right.)

"When did you say you were here before?"

"Three times! First in August; that's when they operated on my tumor . . ."

Grief, she said the word! For a moment I didn't realize that to her it was just a word.

". . . the second time in October for my shunts. And then

at Christmas when my shunt got clogged, like this time. Both times it's been my left shunt. You know what my brothers call me?"

"What?"

"Rube Tube! Rube because I was bald—though some of my hair is coming back now, thank goodness! And Tube because of the tubes in my head. They're so funny. Rube Tube! Can you imagine?"

We laughed. She was unreal. Totally unreal.

"Riann, if you want to say prayers at bedtime here in the hospital and your mother has to leave early or something, I'd enjoy saying prayers with you."

"Really? Oh, good! Mommy does have to leave early sometimes, because of Allison and Kevin and Eric. I usually just say prayers by myself then. But I'd much rather say them with you. I'll ask Mommy to bring the Seagram's bag." Giggle.

"OK."

"She's gone already tonight. And I think I'm ready to go to sleep. Can we say prayers now?"

"Sure."

"You go first."

She folded her hands and bowed her head. I went first.

Then she thanked God for a good day and for helping her feel better. And she prayed that a long list of people would have a "good night's sleep."

"Wanna say the 'Our Father'?" she asked.

Fortunately I remembered that Catholics stop after "deliver us from evil," and say "trespasses" rather than "debts."

(I have heard Riann say the "Our Father" maybe fifty times now. But from that very first time on, I haven't been able to say it once—not once—without thinking of her, without hearing her voice. I wonder how long that will last. It's like a crystal bell ringing.)

I gave her a kiss good-night, turned out the light.

"Leave the door open, please."

"OK."
"Nina . . ."
"Yes?"
"Thank you."

Riann and I said prayers together a few times
more, took a few walks together, talked about her brothers
and sister, about school. She never asked questions. What
eight-year-old do you know who never asks questions? Most
of her sentences began "I remember one time when . . ." Or,
"Do you know what Kevin did one time?" Giggle. Or, "I like
to . . ."
She never asked questions. Never.
In the middle of the week after her operation she went
home.

At the end of the week after she went home, she
came back.

11.

I was afraid of Dr. Jenssen—Dr. Ingrid Jens-
sen. She was the head of Neurology at Children's. Neurology
and Neurosurgery patients shared three-north, I finally discovered.
Neurology is "the branch of medicine dealing with the nervous
system and its diseases," according to Webster.

Dr. Jenssen was somewhere in her thirties, blond, attractive, married, mother of two. She always looked at me disapprovingly. I wondered if my skirt was too short or my hair too long or if she just didn't take me seriously.

I had heard good things about her from the nurses: "Kind, sympathetic, exacting doctor, sweet, friendly . . ." So it bothered me even more. I would smile, but the best she seemed to manage was a half-smile back.

The neurologists made rounds, too. I really wanted to go along. I was learning about neurosurgery, learning to read charts and be somewhat forewarned about what to expect with each patient's diagnosis. I was learning the terms. (I was the hit of the party circuit just explaining a shunt!) I wanted to know about neurology. But in no way could I get up the courage to ask Dr. Jenssen if I could go on rounds with the neurologists.

Then something happened that changed her attitude, or at least changed my reading of her attitude, I guess. It was a brave attempt on my part to give her a compliment, one she deserved . . . and her reaction to something I wrote for the parents of one of her patients.

Mark Heller was a handsome little boy, about three, with black hair and blue eyes. His mother was pretty, young, with dark hair and deep-set brown-black eyes. Mark had a private room across from the small waiting room. Mark's mother spent nights at the hospital, sleeping on the daybed in Mark's room. She would bring Mark out into the small waiting room and hold him in her lap in the evenings and talk with me.

We talked about casual things a lot, Mark's mother and I. Mark was Dr. Jenssen's patient, so I really didn't know what was wrong with him. I never got to see him on rounds or hear the doctors discussing his symptoms or his tests.

His mother said he had seizures. The doctors didn't know what caused them or how to keep them under control for sure.

But I had never seen Mark have a seizure and I really wasn't quite sure what a seizure was . . .

Other than that, Mark's mother didn't talk much about Mark's condition, just held him and cuddled him and loved him. I held him one time when his mother went to answer a telephone call. He seemed sort of stiff. And he didn't react very much. But he was an adorable little boy.

Each day Mark had a test. Then one day his mother said the results of one test had been sent somewhere in the West. Doctors there would look at them and maybe they'd be able to try some very new medication on Mark that might help. It would take a few days to find out.

I was sitting in the small waiting room talking with several mothers and fathers when Dr. Jenssen and Mark Heller's mother walked by. They went down the hall toward the other wing, then stopped and sat in a window ledge and talked. They talked for quite some time.

I watched out of the corner of my eye. Mark's mother looked sad. Dr. Jenssen put her hand on the girl's shoulder, shook her head, and left. Mark's mother sat a few minutes on the window ledge, then walked back to her room. She looked at me for a moment when she walked by, but she didn't stop. She left the door to her room open. I wasn't sure whether or not to go in. But I did. The open door . . .

"Are you OK?"

She shook her head no.

"Would you rather be alone?"

No again. "Could you please close the door." Choked.

I did.

She was like a little girl, like me the night Ethel Stone died, needing to cry but needing someone to cry on.

I sat down on the daybed beside her and she simply buried her head in my arms and wept . . . and tried to talk at the same time.

"They can't do it . . . it won't help . . . no use . . . they said there's no use . . . won't help. I wanted it to work . . . to try . . . just try . . . it was the last hope . . . last hope. Now there's nothing. They've tried everything . . . nothing more . . . they can't do anything more . . .

"How can I tell Barry . . . my husband . . . how can I tell him?"

She sat back, blew her nose, wiped her eyes. The worst was over. And just beginning.

"Is that what Dr. Jenssen was telling you now?"

"Yes. She tried to be nice. But she said the doctors in the West said the new medication won't help Mark . . . He's incurable."

It took everything inside her to form the word *incurable.*

"All we can do now is take him home."

I looked at Mark. He was asleep in his crib, eyes closed, hair tousled, light perspiration on his forehead, little blue sleepers with firemen on them. No wonder it hurt. He *looked* so normal, so healthy, so cute when he was asleep.

"He wasn't like this from the beginning. He was so normal . . . for a whole year. Nothing wrong . . ."

Then the entire story—the story which she had been afraid that verbalizing would somehow negate the last hope—came out, now when there was no "last hope" to tease the superstition.

"One day he had a seizure—just like that, out of the blue. It scared me, but the doctor said just to watch him. Then he had another one six weeks later, and another one two weeks later. That one lasted six hours. Six hours. I felt so helpless. My own little baby. And I couldn't do anything. Nothing.

"He hasn't stopped seizing, really, since. He's on lots of medication now, but even that may lose effect sooner or later.

"I don't think he even knows us any more. I hold him and talk to him and kiss him and love him . . . And he doesn't even know I'm his mommy. He'll never know. Never."

She got up and put her forehead down hard on the railing of the crib . . . as if she wanted to bang her head against something in utter desolation. I watched as one of her tears fell from her cheek onto the crib railing and trickled slowly down the metal bar.

I heard how Mark Heller's mother felt. I saw how Mark Heller's mother felt. Never, never could I, in those moments, *know* how Mark Heller's mother felt.

But seeing and hearing were enough.

"How do you think your husband will take it?"

"He'll try to be brave because of me. He always is. I love him for that. But I know how it hurts him inside.

"But there's something more. Something I'm even more afraid to tell him." She measured out the words as if talking in rhythm with a metronome. "Dr. Jenssen said since she and the other doctors can't determine what caused Mark's seizures, they can't be sure the cause isn't genetic. Which means we can't be sure if we had another baby it wouldn't develop the same thing. So she suggested we not have any more babies maybe . . .

"And Barry and I wanted five children." The tears came again. "We both wanted five children. We decided that the day we got engaged. We've built our lives around that. Even moved to a suburb we didn't especially want to live in just because we could afford a down payment on a bigger house . . . with more bedrooms . . .

"And Barry's father. He can't even admit there's anything wrong with Mark. He talks to him and plays with him and brings him toys . . . even though he never responds. He says it's a 'phase' he's going through. He's sixty-two years old. He has to know better. But he won't admit it. He's his first grandchild.

"And the neighbors. They look at Mark funny when I take him out. I hate that. I guess you can't blame them. We haven't lived there long. They don't know. But they're so obvious. All I want to do is take him for a walk, for some air. Just leave us alone.

"Now it won't change. Sooner or later I'll have to tell them. They'll build it up, too. I hate that. If they just wouldn't look, would just leave us alone. 'Can't he walk yet?' 'Can't he talk yet?' 'How old *is* he?' 'Well, some children are just slower than others. He'll come along soon.'

"Just leave us alone!

"My mother said we'd have to put him in a home if they couldn't give him the medication. I can't think about that yet. Just an hour ago I still had hope. I can't put him away, not in an hour. I want him at home. I don't care. Barry understands. He says I don't have to put him anywhere I don't want to. Do you think I should put him in a home?"

Pause. "I think that's something you may consider at some

future time. But I don't think now is the time."

"But do you think he'll have to be placed someday?"

"I'm not a doctor, so I don't know. But I can see you love Mark very much, which means you want the best for him, that you want him to be as happy and comfortable as possible under the circumstances. As long as that is with you and your husband in your home, then that's the place he should be. But if the time should come that you couldn't care for him properly, for one reason or another, you might want to consider placing him. But I don't think you have to rush into anything. Look at some homes after a while. Talk with staff. See the children. See if they look happy and cared for and loved. Take your time."

"If I were *sure* he didn't know us, absolutely sure, it wouldn't be quite as hard . . . someday. But I wouldn't want him to think we'd abandoned him."

"Yes, I can understand that. But sometimes children are happy, too, with other children in a place equipped to their needs. I'll tell you a story one of the parents here told me one time.

"He had a cousin who was retarded. The parents of the cousin had kept the boy home until he was sixteen, and they just couldn't handle him any more. Finally they placed him—with great fear. All the while they worried they hadn't done the right thing.

"But then the child came home for Christmas vacation. One day the parents saw him sitting unhappily by the Christmas tree. They asked him what was wrong. 'Mommy, Daddy, I love you but when can I go home? I want to see Billy and Freddie . . .'

"The boy was so happy where he had been placed that he called it 'home.' And rather than being hurt, the parents were happy because it made them sure they had done the right thing for the boy they loved.

"It's hard to know what's best all the time. But you love Mark. You'll know if the time comes to place him. I'm not worried about that."

"I guess so. I just have to keep telling myself this is it. We go home. This is it. I guess I still really don't believe it. I guess I still

expect Dr. Jenssen to come through the door and say, 'I made a
mistake. We *can* treat Mark.' But I guess, too, I know she won't.
I think I knew that all along. I guess I want to pray now."

We did.

Mark Heller went home the next day.

That evening I wrote something for his mother . . . I guess for
his mother . . .

"My name is Mark.

When you look at me,
You will measure me
    . . . by my awareness
    . . . by my response
    . . . by my age
    . . . by my development
And you will shake your head
And find me lacking.

But, for me, you are measuring
With the wrong cup.
For I have one possession
Which brims and overflows
Beyond all others.

I have my parents' love.

This cup they give me holds also their
    . . . agony and helplessness
    . . . waiting and hoping
    . . . tears and pain
    . . . aloneness and fear.

But in the end, all these are swallowed up
In the deepness of their love
Which now, in each same moment,
Both lets me go
And will never let me go.

So measure me, if you must . . .
But measure me, too, with my cup
And you will find me
Full."

I saw Dr. Jenssen in the hall a few days later. I got up my courage. "Dr. Jenssen, I just wanted to tell you how much it helped the way you talked with Mark Heller's mother, the way you took the time to explain things. It made my job so much easier. She obviously understood what you were telling her and all the implications."

What I wanted to say didn't come out very well. But Dr. Jenssen still frightened me.

"Yes. She told me on the telephone that you wrote something for her. She liked it very much. What was it?"

"Just something I felt Mark might have said some day if he could. I'll show you a copy if you like."

"Yes. I would."

I got the feeling she thought I had given a medical diagnosis.

"His mother was worried about placing him," I ventured.

"I know. That is a hard decision." And she disappeared into the elevator.

"That was very good. What you wrote for Mark Heller's mother."

It was two days later. I had left a copy of the poem for Dr. Jenssen at the nursing station. She returned it as we passed in the hall. And that did it, I guess. Something did it. The next thing I knew, Dr. Jenssen was showing me photographs of her children and I was asking her if I could go on rounds with the neurologists.

"Yes, of course. But I thought you only made rounds with the neurosurgeons . . ."

How funny. She apparently thought I didn't want to make

rounds with the neurologists. And I thought she didn't want me to . . .

Mark Heller died that fall. At home. Pneumonia.

12.

One of the first things I began to suspect was that "why?" cannot be answered, and that deep down inside, most people know that already. "Why?" theologically, that is.

It can be said what "why?" is not. Mary Smith does not have a tumor because the sins of the first generation are being visited on the third generation. At least not "sins" when they equal immoral or evil acts, as they do in the minds of most people. If that were the case, then Mary Smith would be merely a puppet in the hands of an evil "god."

Mary Smith does not have a tumor because her mother didn't go to Sunday school or her father had an extramarital affair. Not an eye for an eye, a tooth for a tooth. Some people might believe that. But I don't believe that. I don't believe in a puppeteer God.

Most theological conversations—the unscheduled type held while sitting in the little waiting room area with two or three parents dropping in and out—began with, "The first thing I asked myself was 'why? Why did this happen to my child? What did *I* do wrong?' I still think about it every now and then, but I know there's no answer. And intellectually I know God doesn't really work that way. But still you've gotta think every now and then, 'Was it me?'"

I point out that that's a normal reaction. And I reaffirm that

"no, the God I believe in really doesn't work that way, either."
And I reaffirm that "no, it wasn't your sins."

It works, of course. And it's comforting. After all, I wear the
reversed collar, don't I?

But it still doesn't answer the question, "Why?"

But then, I still wouldn't admit to asking it . . . admit to myself.
And I wouldn't admit, either, to a streaking wonder if it wasn't
all a cheap game.

                 I don't remember the first time I saw Joey Col-
lins, or my first conversation with his mother. But I know I saw
them both a lot.

They were in and out of the hospital nine times between
January and May. I say "they" because though Joey wasn't in a
private room, his mother came at ten every morning and stayed
until eight-thirty every evening. Joey's father didn't like hospitals,
so he didn't come as often. But he loved his kid. Joey and his
mother were lucky that way, I guess. A lot of fathers don't
. . . love their kids like Joey, I mean.

Joey had myelomeningocele and hydrocephalus. Myelomeningocele is a birth defect, cause unknown. It's the worst form of
spinabifida. But you almost never hear "spinabifida" around University Children's. It's "myelomeningocele"—which is what most
children we got had. Helping a child with myelomeningocele
takes the most intricate neurosurgical procedures.

When a child is born with myelomeningocele (hereafter referred to as "m-m," as it is at Children's) it means a severe
malformation of nervous tissue and that a portion of the spinal
column is open and protruding, usually covered only by a thin
membrane which may rupture and provide an entry for an infection. (Thus the need for immediate surgery.) The lower this
opening is on the child's back, usually the better it is for the child.
For years, the mortality rate for m-m children was very high.
Doctors simply didn't know how to treat it. But finally a surgical

procedure for m-m was developed and perfected.

The surgery performed immediately on the child with m-m is surgery to close the opening in the child's back. Nerve endings, muscle tissue, and spinal cord tissue are involved, so it's a very delicate, very tedious operation. Every nerve that can be saved is important, because it may make a difference in whether or not the child will ever walk . . . whether with crutches, braces, or if lucky, by himself. Very few m-m children walk unaided. And not that many more can walk at all. But it's a hope their parents cling to.

Once the m-m wound is closed, the child is placed stomach down on a wooden board called a "gingerbread board"—because it looks like a gingerbread man without a head, I guess. The child is cared for on that board until the back wound is healed.

(Does the word *wound* sound strange? It did to me for a long time. But it's standard hospital terminology for any skin opening, whether inflicted by nature, a gunshot, or a surgeon's knife.)

Once the child's m-m wound is healed, all problems are over, other than walking? No.

Usually m-m children don't have bladder or bowel control. In an infant, that doesn't hit home right away. After all, it's normal. But the day comes . . .

Often m-m children have trouble with their hips—they come out of their sockets. So they may have to spend months in a cast.

At times m-m children are born with club feet—more time in casts, more surgery.

And at least eighty percent of the time m-m children develop hydrocephalus.

Surprised? Remember CSF—cerebrospinal fluid? I mentioned that it is a fluid that circulates within the ventricular system (the four cavities) and over the surface of the brain, continuously? And that hydrocephalus was caused by an increase in CSF, in intraventricular pressure, and in intraventricular size?

Well, when the m-m is repaired and the skin closed, very often this brings on an increase in pressure, an increase in CSF, and an increase in intraventricular size—all leading to hydrocephalus.

And sometimes the hydrocephalus is present even before the wound is closed, even before birth. Cause, again unknown.

So the m-m child has another surgery, to insert a shunt to drain off the excess CSF and keep the head from growing.

All of which means that though children born with myelomeningocele will probably never have to have another surgery on their spines, they can spend weeks and months in the hospital for orthopedic work, urology work, and shunt revisions . . . year after year after year . . .

Joey Collins was three when I met him. Most of his hospitalizations during the time I was at Children's were for shunt revisions. The neurosurgeons just couldn't seem to get a shunt that would work right for him. Finally they inserted a V-A shunt—that means ventricle to aorta, or head to heart. Usually shunts are V-P—ventricular to peritoneal, or head to stomach. But the V-A shunt worked.

One time when we were talking about ministers and chaplains Mrs. Collins told me what it was like when Joey was born.

"Who expects that! I mean, you plan and pick out clothes and blankets and set up a nursery and all that stuff. Your first kid; you don't expect no trouble. You expect a baby, to bring him home.

"Oh, I'm not saying I never had fears. That's normal as you go along. But myelomeningocele! I'd never heard of it, so how could I worry about it. You know what I mean?

"But they sedated me real good. I didn't know from nothing for days. I almost lost my mind when they told me. Started screaming and yelling.

"I saw Joey. Lots of mothers don't. But he was bad. A lot of m-m kids don't look that bad. But Joey did. He got this hydrocephalus before he was born even. They didn't know if he'd live.

"Anyway, they were afraid of me. I just started to scream. So they kept giving me stuff and giving me stuff to keep me quiet. I was real out of it.

"And when I did come around I didn't want to see nobody, even Joe [her husband]. I mean nobody could do nothing. Nobody could change nothing. I'd have talked with anybody if it would have helped Joey. But I didn't want a lot of people shaking their heads and muttering how sorry they were. It wouldn't do him no good.

"That's how I think I scared the priest out of his collar. God, when I think of it! I really didn't mean to, but I just didn't want to talk to nobody.

"He knocked on the door . . . all in black with his black Bible and his stiff white collar. And he asked me if there was anything he could do. Like he was scared.

"I told him, yeah, there was something he could do. He could get out and leave me alone and never come back.

"And boy did he! He ran like a rabbit. He never came back, neither.

"I didn't mean to do that. If he'd have come back I'd have apologized. But I was really out of it. And, well, he couldn't have done anything.

"It's been that way up here, too. You're the first chaplain I've ever really talked to. And that's because you don't push in. Before you came, every time we'd see a chaplain coming—those of us who 'live' up here—we'd run into our rooms and close the door. They never stayed. All they'd want to do was come in and say a prayer and leave. On their time, at their convenience. We didn't all feel like praying when they did, that's all.

"But you stay, and you seem to know when somebody wants to just joke and kid around and when somebody wants to be serious. Maybe it's because you're a woman. I don't know."

Maybe that's one reason why I liked Mary Collins. *She* always made *me* feel good! It helps to get a booster shot now and again.

There isn't any end to Joey Collins' story. It will go on and on.

He'll be back for shunt revisions. He'll be back for ortho work. He'll be back for urology work . . .

He has learned to maneuver a wheelchair. Maybe he'll be able to maneuver leg braces. That's his mother and father's hope . . .

He's a cute kid. And I love him.

He just turned four.

Why the "hell," God? Why the four years of hell? Why the ten or twenty or thirty more to come?

Why?

13.

Even when I wasn't on call I had begun going to Children's at least one weekend day. I told myself this was because there were a number of admissions over the weekend and I would get behind if I didn't take that opportunity to meet some of the patients and their families. It was true. But I really just *wanted* to go. That was the greater truth.

Doctors and nurses usually were more relaxed on the weekends. There was time to talk and learn to know each other. I was learning a lot about neurosurgery, and neurology now, too. And the more I knew, the better able I was to keep at least a half-jump ahead in trying to be in the right place at the right time as far as my work with parents was concerned. It really did make a difference, knowing what possible medical situations to expect.

But that Saturday in February I didn't expect to see Riann Miles.

Riann's shunt had stopped working. The same one that had stopped before. Dr. Verdi was out of town. Dr. Praeder had taken Riann to surgery. It was Dr. Praeder who had said he thought her tumor was growing the last time she was in.

I went to the surgery waiting room. Riann's parents were there. It was the first time I had had a chance to talk with her father. He talked about business, about brokerage firms and the stock market.

In about an hour, Dr. Praeder came out in his surgical greens. Riann was all right, in the recovery room. But he did think the tumor was growing. He said it out loud, to her parents, kindly. But that was only his "suspicion." He would talk with Dr. Verdi when he returned on Monday. But for now, Riann was all right.

That's what her father heard: "All right." It was as if Dr. Praeder hadn't said another word; had never mentioned "tumor" or "growing." He didn't hear it. He simply didn't hear it. He couldn't hear it.

It was late. Riann's father wanted to go home. Riann was all right, he repeated. And she would be "out of it" for the rest of the evening, he rationalized. He wanted to go home.

Mrs. Miles didn't. But she didn't say so. She understood. No, not understood—accepted. It would take months for her to understand.

They went home.

But I couldn't go home. Riann didn't need me. But I needed to see her, needed to see her back in her room and tucked in for the night, needed some completion to the day, to tie up the ends.

I went into the recovery room—Intensive Care on Saturdays —and sat on a small stool by the head of her bed. Actually, she was still on the surgical cart because in about an hour, when they were sure she was all right, she would be moved back to her room on the neurosurgical floor.

I remember sitting there and looking at her. Intensive Care is one large room with about nine beds and two isolation areas. It is very, very bright, all the time. I've never seen the lights turned down in Intensive Care. And with the white sheets, the glare is almost blinding, especially at night.

Riann's head was shaved, again. And she had one of those multicolored blood pressure cuffs on her arm, like Marilee Johnson.

She was naked, covered loosely by a sheet. The doctors had inserted a urinary catheter with a plastic collection bag hooked to the side of her bed. There were reddish-brown sterile wash marks on her neck, left over from surgery. And spots of blood, too, here and there.

She was restless, kept kicking off the sheet and lying there naked. It's a very inhuman, depersonalizing thing—a little girl lying naked with her head shaved and bandaged, with a urinary catheter sticking out and a blood pressure cuff wrapped around and an I.V. tube sticking in. I wanted to yank out all the tubes and wrap her in the sheet and make her hair grow long and throw away the bandages and hold her in my arms and say "everything will be all right."

But I just sat there and watched.

The nurse came and took her temperature, rectally, and her blood pressure. She talked with her, trying to arouse her. There was a slight response. "Not yet," said the nurse, "but soon."

About twenty minutes later the nurse was satisfied. Riann was answering questions coherently. But she was still very drowsy. That's normal. She was all right.

"Do you want your mommy?" asked the nurse.

"Yes." Then Riann dropped off to sleep again.

"Her parents have gone," I whispered to the nurse. No further mention was made. Riann didn't remember.

I helped push her down to three-north on the surgical cart. I tucked her in . . . tied my loose ends . . . and went home.

But I had heard Dr. Praeder.
So had Riann's mother.

The following Thursday they performed another
surgery on Riann—a craniotomy.

Tests proved the tumor had grown. Dr. Praeder's "suspicion"
was right. Dr. Verdi would try to get as much of it as he could.
Maybe he could get it all.

At Children's they had "play ladies." Jane was the play lady on
three-north. She was in her mid-twenties, cute, enthusiastic. Play
ladies wore bright-colored smocks and came around every afternoon to play with the children, all the children who were well
enough to get up and gather at the end of the hall in a small play
area. On three-north the play area was at the opposite end of the
L-shaped wing from the parents' smoking/waiting area.

Jane was attached to Riann, too. The afternoon before Riann's
surgery, Jane had an ice cream party for the children on three-
north. She brought an electric freezer and all the ingredients. The
children helped make the ice cream and then Jane played records
while the mixture was churning. The children loved it. "But I did
it for Riann," said Jane. I knew.

The one thing Riann hated above all else was "needles." Most
children are that way. They can be picked at and probed at and
X-rayed and bandaged, but needles are a no-no.

With Riann the fear was acute. She'd start to cry before the
syringe was even filled. Just the sight of a needle set her off. It
was the same when they wanted to draw blood.

I was in her room the day before surgery when they drew blood.
She held onto my arms and hands, and screamed. I remember
trying to get her mind off what was going on by asking her
questions about other things. It didn't work. She screamed and
sobbed and trembled until the bed shook.

Needle pricks for blood samples really don't hurt that much.
But if you're afraid of needles, the mere word hurts. Especially

if you've been a human pincushion for the last eight months of
your life.

A volunteer with a lot of fourteen-carat gold bracelets and
diamond rings brought a puppet theater into Riann's room after
the ice cream party. The puppets acted out what would happen
prior to surgery. It was a good idea, so children wouldn't be totally
uninformed or unprepared for what was to happen to them the
following day.

Other children crowded around Riann's bed to watch. Riann
had seen it all before, before her first operation last August. But
she politely didn't interrupt. Her mother arrived in the middle of
the skit. She watched politely, too. But she was terribly on edge,
as if she wanted everyone to "clear out" and leave her alone with
Riann.

But they didn't get a chance to be alone all afternoon. People
paraded in and out: visitor people, nurse and doctor people, technician people, a priest to give communion. It was after dinner
until Riann and her mother got to be alone.

It was important, to be alone together . . . because Mrs. Miles
couldn't spend the night with Riann. Not because the child didn't
have a private room; she did. But because Mr. Miles wanted his
wife home that night.

Whether or not to spend the night with Riann despite her
husband's wishes was my first real discussion with Mrs. Miles. It
had agonized her for days before the operation. She wanted to
stay. I know I would have wanted to stay if Riann had been my
daughter. There are no guarantees in brain surgery. She could die.
No guarantees.

What would I do if I were in her place, Mrs. Miles asked.

I was in the middle. I thought I knew well what I would do:
stay. But I couldn't say that. So I just listened. "I don't know your
husband or his reasons for wanting you home tonight well enough
to answer," was my only response.

I think I did, though, know his reasons . . . remembering how
he had discussed the stock market . . . and hadn't seemed to hear

Dr. Praeder's "suspicion." He couldn't divorce himself from the norm. And the norm was having his wife at home at night. He was still in shock, still denying. As if by denying the seriousness of Riann's tumor it would go away.

Mrs. Miles knew his reasons, too. "They'll give Riann something to make her sleep early anyway," she rationalized aloud. "And we'll be here first thing in the morning. She'll be all right."

But it bothered her, gnawed at her.

Me too.

Mrs. Miles's sister spent that pre-surgery night with Riann. She flew in from California. (Did you think I would offer? The relationship wasn't that close yet. The mutual bond of trust was building, but it hadn't reached that height. My offering to stay would have created another problem, not a solution. It was too soon, on both sides.)

Mrs. Miles and her sister were very close. It was as if someone had released a pressure valve that had been about to burst when Brooke Flynn walked into Riann's room. Mrs. Miles nearly collapsed into her sister's arms.

Mrs. Miles's sister and Riann and I said prayers together that night. We used the "relics" from the Seagram's bag, plus a special one Riann's grandmother had sent from Florida. Riann was very, very tired. It had been a long day. Tomorrow would be short—for her.

Jane, the "play lady," came in early the next day . . . at seven A.M. So did I. Both of us knew why. Neither of us was needed, or could do anything. But we couldn't stay home.

I went with Mrs. Miles's sister to bring coffee to Riann's room for her parents. I stuck my head in the door just long enough to hand in the coffee and say hi. Only the small night light over Riann's bed was on. Her mother and father were standing close, talking with her. The room was eerie. Maybe the room wasn't eerie at all. Maybe it was what was happening that was eerie.

Riann showed me some little stuffed animals a friend had sent her. I said they were cute. But I didn't stay. It wasn't a party.

I went and sat in the little waiting room and smoked.

I wanted to be a full-fledged Catholic priest. The Mileses were Catholic; and I felt that if I had been a Catholic priest I could have done something more, been more helpful. Right then I felt like a rookie sitting on a log. Riann deserved more than a student chaplain.

But in my anger, I turned the coin over. So, I was on the outside and helpless to effect change. Big deal. In the long run, when the chips are down, a tumor is a tumor is a tumor . . . and what good is a chaplain? Any chaplain?

A blond nurse came by with a surgical cart. It was time. I heard Riann cry a little bit. Then I remembered she had to have a pre-surgery shot. The nurse came out of the room for a few minutes; gave them a little bit longer. Then she went back in.

The sheet was pulled high around Riann's neck as the nurse pushed her by on the surgery cart. And she looked so tiny and afraid. But her right arm wiggled out from under the sheet and she waved and smiled as a tear dripped on her pillow. "Bye, Nina."

I watched them go down the hall. Her mother and father walking along beside her.

I watched her mother and father return alone. He got his hat and coat, "to take a walk." Mrs. Miles and her sister and I all sat and smoked. Mrs. Miles and her sister didn't normally smoke. But they needed something to do with their hands, some rote motion in which to engage, I guess. There was nothing else normal. We didn't say much.

I had breakfast later with Jane, the "play lady." She had stayed with Riann outside the surgery door until the little girl had to go in . . . alone.

How we all fight helplessness.

How helpless we are.

Creature, not creator.

But *we* would have done a better job of it, now, wouldn't we? Or is that the very reason for this world?

Riann had come out of surgery by two-thirty that afternoon. She was all right, in the recovery room. But Dr. Verdi had called her parents into his office to talk.

Earlier Dr. Praeder had told me Dr. Verdi couldn't get all the tumor . . . just a tiny piece. It had spread too far too fast. They had suspected that all along. After all, they hadn't been able to get it the first time, he said; why should this time be any different?

"But it was big," said Dr. Praeder. "Bigger than I thought."

Nobody told me about their faces, the faces of patients who have had craniotomies; what happens to them. So I didn't know.

I saw Riann in the neurosurgery Constant Care room that evening. She was actually awake and talking when the nurse brought her down from the recovery room. I couldn't believe it. She sat up for a bit, looking at flowers and cards she had received.

"She's fine," said her father. He stayed with her longer than usual. She really looked bright.

But the next morning I didn't recognize her. Her face looked like a basketball with black eyes. "Oh, that's normal," said Mary Cooke. "People's faces always swell like that after a craniotomy. I guess nobody warned you. It is a shock the first time. You see, they pull the skin the whole way down off the forehead and . . ."

"That's OK, Mary. I'd rather not hear 'why' right now. As long as it's normal."

She laughed. "Yeah, it's normal. It'll go down in a few days. Don't worry."

Riann was pretty well out of it for the next two or three days. The swelling was incredible. Her eyes were swollen shut and almost blocked from view by the swelling above and below.

Every now and then she'd forget where she was. She thought she was at school one time, at ballet class another time.

But mostly she slept. And managed to cry when the nurses had to give her her shots. And oh how the nurses hated to do it.

For Jennifer Bradford it was hardest of all. Jennifer was the P.M. charge nurse, from three-thirty to eleven-thirty . . . or twelve-thirty . . . or one. I was around more and more in the evenings, so I got to know her better. She was a central casting nurse: tall, slender, fresh-faced, well-manicured hands, very clean, and very efficient. But she would just agonize when she'd have to give Riann a shot.

One evening there were two shots ordered for the same time. "I just don't want to do this. She's hurting so much anyway. I just don't want her to have to cry again. Why couldn't I be off tonight?" Jennifer Bradford wasn't profuse about it; very quiet. She kept busy. Gave other medications to other children. But the two syringes wouldn't go away. They stared back at her from the medicine cart when there were no more pills to give.

I saw her go sit in the little room behind the nursing station and hold her stomach, trying to be inconspicuous. But finally she did it. What else could she do? And Riann cried and cried.

Jennifer didn't say much the rest of the evening.

That was when I realized the difference in our jobs. Jennifer —the nurses—had the worst bargain. I could care about the children and talk with them and try to comfort them and try to help. The nurses could care about the children and talk with them and try to comfort them and try to help—but they also had to hurt. They had to give shots and medicines and enemas and wound scrubs. They couldn't just be nice. And that was worse. I could be nice all the time.

No wonder Jennifer got so angry one evening when a doctor told a complaining child, "Wait a minute, I'm not going to hurt you. I never give you shots or pills. The nurses do that. They hurt you; I don't. Don't get upset with me."

No, being a chaplain is easier.

Except for that one question. "Why?"

It was happening. I was beginning to ask those questions. The gnawing of "Why evil, why pain?" was getting greater. "God won't let her suffer more than she can stand . . . He may have foreseen a life of constant agony and pain . . . and because he loved her so much . . ." Those answers alone weren't sufficient —for my gut as well as my mind—any more.

Fortunately—and this has never happened yet—I didn't withdraw from God. I didn't renounce him. But I was beginning to question, beginning to need a "theology" that would get me through these questions, my own questions. Maybe it would be a theology too deep to be used outright in crisis conversations with parents; but I needed a theology that would get me through three A.M. in bed awake . . . wrestling with the "why?" that now came between the mental slide pictures.

That theology became increasingly necessary as I got to know Riann Miles and Alex Felini better.

14.

Alex Felini got a brainstem cyst for his seventh birthday. It's called a posterior fossa cyst. Just like Marilee Johnson had. Oh, he had the cyst before his birthday; that's just the day it was diagnosed.

I hadn't paid much attention to Alex Felini when he first came in. In fact, he had had a shunt inserted to relieve the pressure from the cyst before I even met him.

That was my fault. Lindsay Grice was admitted on the day of Riann's surgery. I was actually glad. I needed her. Can you imagine? But I was glad, nonetheless. I held her for hours that evening. She was in for another shunt revision.

But between Riann and Lindsay and the others I already knew, I just couldn't handle one patient more right away. I knew Alex was there and I felt appropriately guilty; but I would make up excuse after excuse to myself not to get acquainted yet. Maybe subconsciously I suspected he would be there for a while.

He was: for over five months, with the exception of one week.

"A cyst is usually benign, isn't it?" I asked Mary Cooke one day after I had finally met Alex Felini and his parents. In fact, Alex was in surgery right then.

"Yes, but don't count on that meaning anything. I don't want to be cynical, but I've been here long enough. It seems we have much more trouble with kids with benign cysts than with brain tumors. I hope Alex will be all right; but I'm not banking on it."

What a pessimist, I thought.

Mary Cooke was right. Alex Felini had every complication in the book, and some not in the book.

Alex's mother and father, Carrie and Tony, lived in the same neighborhood where both had grown up. They had two other children, Chrissy, who was four, and Sandi, who was five, and tons of relatives. I got to know them all.

But it was several days after Alex's first surgery—for the cyst —that we talked together at length, his family and I. I had copped out until then.

Carrie Felini's father was a construction worker, a heavy equipment operator. He would sit there in the small waiting room and look at me. "You really a minister?"

"I'm a student chaplain, studying to be a minister."

"Not a priest?"

"No. The Catholic Church doesn't ordain women."

"Yeah, that's what I thought. How come you wanna do that?"

"I don't know for sure."

"Seems strange, I mean for a girl. Can you get married? Have kids?"

"Sure, both."

"Don't you wanna?"

"Sure."

"Then whatchya doin' here? I mean, it's nice and all, but what about having your own family?"

"I want to someday. But it just hasn't happened."

"You probably got too high standards. No man can live up to all them standards some women holds."

"Yes, you're probably right at that. My standards probably are too high." Though I was sure not in the way Carrie's father meant.

"Take my advice. You're a pretty girl, really OK. Get a guy while you're still pretty. It'll change, ya know. Everybody gets older. Get one while you can!"

I could feel myself shriveling up and bursting with wrinkles and arthritis while I sat there!

"You know, I'm gonna buy a St. Jude candle for Alex." It was one of Tony Felini's sisters. She sat down beside us.

"We have a St. Jude candle in the chapel, I think. Actually, it's just the glass candle holder, but I'm sure I could fix it with a candle if you'd like."

"You're the chaplain, aren't you? Carrie was telling me there was a woman chaplain up here."

"Yes." We introduced ourselves.

"Yeah, I'd really like a St. Jude candle, if you could put it in the chapel."

"Sure."

"You know, Alex isn't doing so good. They say they may have to take him back to surgery. His neck is all swollen and puffy where they operated."

"Do they mean tonight?"

"Maybe. The doctor—Dr. Praeder—is in with him now."

They took Alex back to surgery at six-thirty that evening. The wound was infected. It burst pus. Then they took him back to surgery at ten that night. Opened his stomach, trying to find something. I guess his fever was still up. They didn't find anything.

I put the St. Jude candle in the chapel between surgeries. I met Carrie's sister in the hall and told her. "Oh good, thank you. Can we go there now and pray for Alex?"

We did.

Just after we finished and were sitting on the little chairs in the chapel watching the lighted St. Jude candle, Alex's parents and grandfather came in and sat down. They prayed silently, and then we talked for a few minutes.

"Well," said Alex's grandfather, "you said you were a chaplain, didn't you?"

"Yes."

"Well, let's pray for Alex. That's what we're here for."

Tony Felini's sister tried to apologize . . . to say I had just done that. But I said I'd like to again.

After the prayer Carrie Felini looked up at me. "Gee, thank you. You done that just as well as any priest I ever heard. I mean . . . not that you ain't as 'good' as a priest . . . just that we, being Catholic, never knew . . ."

I knew what she meant. It was the best compliment I had gotten since I had been at Children's.

Alex Felini turned out to be a funny kid. Even when he wasn't feeling very good, he could still be funny.

One night Dr. Praeder was particularly worried about Alex. The little boy hadn't really been physically right since surgery: infection, fever, chills, headache. He just wasn't progressing as well as he should.

Dr. Praeder: "Alex, I love you so much. Alex, you have to get better, Alex. Alex, I love you so much. Alex, you are such a sweet boy. You have to feel better, Alex. I love you so much."

Alex: "Yeah, you're OK, too, Maxmillian."

The nurse who was in Alex's room at the time almost dropped the I.V. bottle laughing. From then on, all Dr. Praeder got from the staff was, "You're OK, too, Maxmillian!"

Another evening I was walking toward the nursing station when I heard laughter coming from the Constant Care room. Several nurses and Dr. McMahan were standing around Alex's bed. The little boy had been having trouble urinating on his own, and that was one of the requirements for him to be discharged from the Constant Care room to his own room. This was after the fourth or fifth surgery for one complication or another.

Finally, a tiny bit of urine flowed. Alex was exhausted. "But that ain't all, Doc. I really gotta go a lot. Rub some more, nurse."

"Alex, I think I'm going to have to insert a catheter. This just isn't working," said Dr. McMahan.

"OK, Doc. Whatever you say, 'cause I really gotta go!"

Dr. McMahan attached a catheter to a urine bag and then inserted it. It worked.

"Ah," said a relieved Alex. "Now, Doc, that's the *real* thing! That's the real thing!"

We still laugh about that. That and "You're OK, too, Maxmillian," and so many many others . . .

15.

Suddenly I didn't want to go to Europe. If anyone had told me the previous November that that would be the case, I would have laughed him out of the room. I love Europe. I think part of me always will see the Swiss Alps across the meadow from Interlaken's Grand Hotel Victoria-Jungfrau, or live by a tiny lake in Welsh Snowdonia.

But by March, with enough money and enough time to chew

and digest Europe in a long, leisurely, comfortable meal . . . I
didn't want to go. I wanted to stay on three-north at University
Children's Hospital, and to be there completely . . . not have to
make a pretense of liking to go to my general medical floor at
Adult Hospital.

Under normal circumstances, that would have been impossible, staying at Children's. Normally, another group of students
would have been arriving. But this March that wasn't the case.
There was no spring quarter of CPE. No new students would
arrive until June.

So I asked Craig Hatfield if I could stay. After making me
sweat it out, he said yes.

And that "yes" of Craig Hatfield's, and those two and one half
months made all the difference. They confirmed for me that I
wanted to be a hospital chaplain. They added depth and dimen-
sion to my theological probings. And they confirmed, for me, the
crying need for chaplains with concern and training—and time
—to work on a long-term basis with critically and terminally ill
children and their families.

I wouldn't have traded those two and one half months for one
hundred trips to Europe.

The St. Jude candle we placed for Alex Felini was the patriarch
of generations of daily St. Jude candles. Then one day Alex's aunt
said she had found weekly St. Jude candles at a religious goods
store and had bought several. Thus began the second succession
. . . these changed each week.

If people always got what they wanted by praying profusely,
Alex Felini would have had one surgery and gone home to play.
Rarely in those weeks between the end of February, when Alex
was admitted, and June 6, the day I left Children's, did I ever go
into the chapel without seeing a member of the Felini clan praying for Alex.

But it was hardest for Tony, Alex's father. At first he wouldn't
come to the chapel often. But as time went on, he began to try
to pray Alex well. It seemed to become a test of his ability to

convince God of his sincerity through prayer. At times the prayer tension was so great that I felt if God didn't come through and "let Alex get well," Tony Felini would punch Him in the teeth.

But nothing changed. It was like a merry-go-round. One week Alex was up and about, six-guns tugging his pajama bottoms. The next week he made another trip to surgery: drain the wound, exploratory laparotomy, one shunt, two shunts, fix a shunt, no shunts, burr holes to relieve pressure, on and on and on.

And each time, *telling* Alex he had to make yet another trip to the fifth floor operating room got more and more difficult. "Don't-get-emotionally-involved" Maxmillian Praeder was getting just that. For he was Alex's principal neurosurgeon. And he began to see it as a personal war, too. After all, Alex had a benign, posterior fossa cyst. He shouldn't be having all these complications. But the Felinis, rightly, never lost faith in Dr. Praeder.

Each time Alex had surgery he snapped back. After the initial surgery it had been a long, long pull. But from there on in, he just snapped back. It was like diving off a diving board and bobbing back up again. Except in this case Alex had to be dragged back to the board each round. And it began doing something to his morale, not surprisingly.

After the eighth surgery it looked like things had worked. Alex seemed all right. But the angiogram showed pressure. They had to put in a shunt. Just *one more* surgery. Better to do it now than send Alex home and have to bring him back in a week. That's what they decided. But Dr. Praeder was agonizing over telling Alex.

"How can I tell him that again? I am afraid he can't take it. The ninth time! He is old enough to know what is going on. And I love him so much. It really hurts me."

That was on a Thursday. They were to operate on Friday. On Saturday Alex went to a baseball game with his family. Dr. Praeder just couldn't do it. He had to give Alex that weekend to breathe. Even if it was his last surgery before going home, a few days more wouldn't make much difference. Alex took an eight-hour hospital pass Saturday. They would operate Monday.

I remember the Sunday evening when Dr. Praeder told Alex about that ninth surgery. I was sitting in the waiting area next to Alex's room. I thought the wall between us would crumble.

Dr. Praeder finally emerged from the room, ashen-faced, and hurried off down the corridor. My urge was to follow him. But he wouldn't want me to see the results of his doing what he told me he couldn't allow himself to do. So I stayed.

About an hour later, he found me sitting at the nursing station and asked if I'd like a lift home. As we walked past the little waiting room, there sat Alex and his mother and father. Alex had on his flannel cowboy pajamas and his heavy black wing-tipped shoes. He always wore those heavy shoes. His hair had begun to grow out and was in a soft brown crew cut brushed forward. His eyes were sad, like big chocolate drops ready to melt.

"Dr. Maxmillian . . ."

"Yes, Alex?"

"Dr. Praeder, Alex has something to say to you," said his mother.

"Dr. Maxmillian, I'm sorry I got mad and yelled earlier. My mother and dad explained how you don't really want me to have to have all these operations, but how it has to be if I want to be really well. But I hope you can understand," he added, looking down, "that it still makes me mad."

He said it like a man, the whole thing. But his hands shook quietly on his lap.

"Of course I understand, Alex. Thank you very much. I know that took a lot of courage. You are a very brave young man."

But Alex couldn't say any more. He tried not to cry, but it was beginning. He started scuffing the dangling toes of his shoes back and forth against the floor.

Dr. Praeder could tell. "Thank you," he said again, to all three, then turned back down the hall.

I didn't say a word. He was close to tears. "I don't believe it," he repeated and repeated, shaking his head. "I just don't believe it. Oh, God, why?"

I looked back over my shoulder. Alex and his mother and father still sat in the dimly lighted waiting room.

Too much happened to remember it all, that Monday of Alex's surgery. I don't remember how it began, because so many others had begun the same way: another dive from the high dive, another bob up.

Except it wasn't.

Surgery went all right. I happened to be sitting with the Felinis when Dr. Praeder came out of the O.R. "But we'll have to watch him closely. There was a lot of pressure."

On rounds that evening Alex responded to verbal communication. But he didn't wake up again all evening. I left at about eleven.

When I returned Tuesday morning, Alex was in Intensive Care —on the sixth floor. He had started to become decerebrate. That means, basically, he became rigid. You can't imagine, maybe, just how rigid someone can get.

They had made burr holes—that's four incisions, one in each "corner" of the skull—to relieve the pressure on the brain. Early that Tuesday morning they had made the burr holes: ten surgeries.

When I saw Alex lying there in Intensive Care I just remember getting very cold.

The Felinis were in the chapel. A St. Jude candle was burning. We prayed. We all were in shock. How dare the routine be broken! How dare God "not let" Alex bob back up!

"But Dr. Praeder said this happens sometimes," said Tony Felini. "It's a form of brain swelling. A person with that can be unconscious for a long time . . . But it doesn't mean he will die . . . If the brain swelling reverses he can be fine."

Dr. Praeder repeated the same thing to me later. There was hope. It was bad, but there was hope.

As the day dragged on that Tuesday Alex got worse. They took him to surgery to insert a second shunt: eleven surgeries. He still got worse.

"We'll do an angiogram," said Dr. Praeder. Maybe the shunts aren't working. Maybe we'll find something else." They took Alex to angio. It was about three-thirty in the afternoon.

"Go along?" Alex's father asked me. "If you want to," Alex's mother said. Her voice had changed. I sensed something had snapped. But it wasn't the time to talk . . .

I went to angio. It was a big room with a huge overhead X-ray machine that took a quick, running series of X-ray photos. The whole thing only took a few seconds. It was getting ready that could take hours.

Hollow needles had to be inserted into two arteries in the neck. As each artery was hit, the hollow needles were quickly plugged. *Finding* the two arteries could be tedious and tricky. When all was ready, the needles were unplugged and dye was squirted in through the needles. It circulated through the arterial system in the head. As the dye moved along the arterial path, X-ray photos were taken in quick sequence. The patient was heavily sedated for an angiogram, but general anesthetic usually was not used with children.

In the middle of Alex's angio, as he had one tube-needle in an artery of his neck, Dr. McMahan yelled, "He's going sour! We can't go on. Call the O.R.!"

They raced Alex to the operating room. "Find his parents and tell them I want to talk with them in the six-center waiting room," Dr. Praeder said to me on the run.

I did. And he did. "We have to take out the shunts and put one shunt on the outside," Dr. Praeder explained, "so we can be sure it is working, sure there isn't an infection."

The procedure is called "inserting an EVD"—external ventricular drainage. Instead of the excess CSF draining off into the tummy, it now would drain into a tube sticking out of Alex's head and attached to a clear glass container. That way doctors could measure the amount of CSF draining off into the container and then regulate the pressure. They also could tell by the clearness or opaqueness of the fluid whether or not the CSF was infected.

"OK, OK," said Mrs. Felini. "Anything."

"Will you go with Alex?" asked Mr. Felini.

I nodded. Mrs. Felini said nothing.

I couldn't believe it. When the incisions over the burr holes were opened, there was the brain—almost pushing out, grayish-white. I could see it.

To make a burr hole, the scalp is opened, then a round hole is drilled in the skull. Thus the brain can expand and pressure can be eased. It is through this hole in the skull that I saw the swollen brain.

But when I began to realize that it was *Alex's* swollen brain —I had to leave.

(*And that is all the difference.* That, I was to put together much later, is why a neurosurgeon must guard against getting too "close" to his patient while he [the neurosurgeon] still must operate. In the operating room, for the neurosurgeon, it must be "a" brain, not Alex's brain or Riann's brain.)

I threw my green surgical clothes—gown, mask, hat, and shoes —into their proper "used" bins, and went to the chapel. That was the third surgery I had watched. But it was the first one on a child I knew well. I was sick: exhausted, ineffective, powerless . . . sick. I wanted to be alone.

I was in the chapel five minutes when the Felinis came in. I whispered that surgery was nearly over. But we all prayed our own prayers.

"Will you pray for Alex?" It was Tony Felini.

"Yes! If you really want to pray for him, pray that he dies!" It was Carrie Felini. She was exploding.

I wasn't ready. I wasn't up for it. Her words hit me like a hammer. I didn't say anything at first. Was she right? I couldn't blame her. It seemed so endless, so predetermined, so stacked— the deck against Alex. But die? Pray for that? That Alex would die? Now?

"I'm sorry, but I can't do that," I said. "Not yet. I can't play God yet . . ." It was not the time to argue. But I had to be true to God, to the God I believed in, anyway.

"Oh no!" the voice pierced back, breaking in mid-sentence, angry, cold, sarcastic. "We can't play God. We have to have hope! Hope! Hope! Hope!"

Tony Felini started to cry.

"The time may come when I can pray that he dies. But not now. Not while he's up there fighting. Not while Dr. Praeder says there *is* hope, that the brain swelling could go away." (But as those words came out, the picture of Alex's swollen brain flashed through my mind.) "I'm sorry, Carrie, but I can't. Not now. Not yet."

She didn't say anything.

I started to pray. "Dear God, it's almost unbearable. The agony. We want to flail our arms and scream. At you, at the world, at the unfairness. 'Why?' we ask. *Would* it be better if Alex dies?

"Oh, God, we don't know. Only you know that. But in our unspeakable anger and utter helplessness, give us the faith to trust you.

"Give strength to the doctors. Help them draw on all the skills they know as they work to save Alex.

"And God, above all, please be with Alex. Let him know you love him and are holding on to him. Let him know that his parents love him, that they agonize to see him suffer so. Give Alex strength and love, oh God. And, please, hold onto us . . . to all of us . . . now."

The dam broke . . . about two sentences earlier . . . for Carrie Felini. It all fell out on the needlepoint chapel kneeling cushions with blue butterflies and suns and moons and winds and flowers on them.

And the dam broke for me, too. I've never known whether that was the "right thing" or the "wrong thing" for a chaplain to do. But I do know it was unavoidable. I sobbed, too. I just couldn't take it any more. The day had been beyond human comprehension, beyond human assimilation—at least my comprehension, my assimilation.

Unexpectedly, Carrie, still crying, came and sat next to me and put her arms around me. Tony followed. And so we sat there, three helpless individuals now a helpless group.

What difference did it make . . . ?

If it ever entered my mind, which it didn't, whether or not I was happier as a chaplain at Children's than I had been in broadcasting, Manuelito Cerci gave me the perfect test.

Manuelito and his parents were from Italy. Dr. Verdi had seen Manuelito on one of his frequent European trips and had told his parents that if they brought the child to Children's there was a chance he could operate successfully on him.

Manuelito had an aneurysm. Basically, that's a mix-up of veins and arteries to the brain. To straighten it out is a very difficult and very delicate operation. Not only does it involve correctly redirecting the blood flow; but there's the danger that while the surgeon is doing that, he'll burst a malformed, ballooning vein or artery.

Correcting an aneurysm can require two surgeries. And usually it is only successful on adults or older children. Manuelito was not yet two. No one that young had ever before lived through aneurysm surgery.

When I met Manuelito and his mother and father the boy had already lived through the first half of this surgery, performed the preceding fall. If he, and Dr. Verdi, made it this time, the procedure would be complete and Manuelito would become the youngest child in medical history to have survived aneurysm surgery. And Dr. Verdi would be a medical hero.

Manuelito's parents didn't speak English. His father, who was a university professor in Italy, was learning. When his mother (who hadn't come to the U.S. for the first surgery) arrived, she spoke only one or two words. But she was determined to learn.

For the first few days, everyone just smiled at her. I wanted to talk with her—as I'm sure everyone else did—but I didn't know any Italian and didn't know for sure if she wanted to try.

But one day she solved the problem. I had on my clerical collar and was sitting in the small waiting room with Mrs. Cerci and some other mothers. During a brief lull in the conversation, Mrs. Cerci looked up a word in her Italian-to-English dictionary, then pointed to my collar and asked, "church?"

I nodded yes.

"Catholic?"—with a tone of disbelief.

"No," I answered. "Presbyterian."

A puzzled look.

I took her dictionary, but the word *Presbyterian* wasn't in it. So I looked up *Protestant.*

"Protestante," I answered.

"Ah, si! Protestante."

I realized the obvious lacking of my Italian pronunciation. She looked up another word.

"Minister?"

"Si," I answered, very proud that I'd picked up Italian for "yes" so quickly.

She looked up another word or two . . . "Protestante . . . minister . . . female?"

"Si."

"No!" Surprise.

"Si."

"Non Catholic?"

"No."

"Si?" She pointed to my ring finger.

"No."

"Oh?"

Then I realized she probably was misinterpreting, thinking I couldn't marry because I was a minister. But how on earth did one say, "I can marry if I wish, but I haven't yet," in Italian? But by that time she had looked up the words.

"Church . . . rule . . . Protestante?"

"No."

She looked up another word. "Personal?"

"Si."

Another word. "Boy friend?" and she pointed to me.

"Si," I laughed, and held up three fingers.

"Bravo!" She seemed happier.

That was the beginning. I bought an English-to-Italian dictionary and began learning Italian for the duration. But she was much better.

It was fun. But it was also tense. The day for Manuelito's surgery grew closer. And Mrs. Cerci—Lana—and her husband got more tense. He would pace the floor for hours and take long walks. She would find me to talk with, just to relieve the tension.

The day before surgery I asked her if she wanted to go to the chapel. Yes, she said; but she wanted to wait to go while Manuelito was in surgery.

It was difficult in the chapel that Thursday. At least I felt so. There was so much I wanted to say, but couldn't. I guess that was selfish in a way. But I soon appreciated the reason for "Our Father" rather than "My Father."

I suppose we did communicate with our eyes, though. She seemed to want to stay a long time. And she kept holding onto my hand as if for me not to go. But how difficult it must have been for her—for both of them—to be in such an isolated situation at such a critical time.

Manuelito had gone into surgery at eight A.M. We went to the

chapel at about ten. And all day long after that, whenever Mrs.
Cerci saw me she would ask if I had heard anything about
Manuelito.

"No," I answered, "I'm sorry. They're still in surgery."

"True? True?" she would always follow.

"True," I assured her.

Then she would tell me she trusted me to always tell her the
truth, no matter what.

I said I would. But my knees would go weak.

At six-thirty I saw Dr. Verdi, in his surgical greens with white,
blood-spattered shoes, race into the Cercis' room on three-north.
Behind him was Dr. Praeder, who simply looked at me and said,
"He's all right. So far, he's all right, Nina, honey."

Knowing the great amount of tension that fell off my shoulders
at that moment, I can't even begin to imagine how much greater
the relief must have been for his parents.

Dr. Verdi left and dashed into a stairwell as I was walking back
down the hall. I hadn't seen his face at all, but I could imagine
he was happy.

"Nina!" Mrs. Cerci was running down the hall toward me.
"He is alive! He is alive! He is all right! Manuelito, he is alive!"
She grabbed me and hugged the breath out of me . . . and started
to cry.

They were still closing Manuelito's wound. It would be nearly
another two hours until his parents could see him in Intensive
Care. They decided to make some telephone calls and then get
a sandwich.

I went to dinner with some nurses from three-north. Just as I
was going in the cafeteria door, Dr. Verdi came around the
corner, still in his scrub suit.

"Nina, honey ["honey" always seemed to be my last name for
both Dr. Verdi and Dr. Praeder], come to my office for a minute,
can you? I have something for you."

I followed him into his office. He reached into his desk drawer
and pulled out a bottle of French perfume. He had been to Paris

a few weeks earlier and had promised to bring me some. I never dreamed he would remember.

But I was more fascinated by his face. I had never seen anything like it. Ever. He had just stood for a good part of twelve hours performing an operation that would make medical history. And his face reflected every moment of the agony, fear, exhilaration and joy that had gone into it. I could barely carry on the amenities. I wanted to remember his face. I still do.

The next day that mental picture of Dr. Verdi's face was so vivid I had to tell him. So I wrote something.

I guarantee you, it is not nearly adequate:

> . . . But in the vacuum of moments just after that surgery,
> I saw what the journals could not see;
> What the textbooks will not record;
> What the surgeon himself cannot understand.

For I glimpsed the mystery of what *life* costs another human being.

> I saw in his eyes,
> In his face,
> In his body,
> The terrible price he pays.

And suddenly, for a moment,
> I touched the reason for the transcendent mystery of God.
Because, for a moment,
> I touched the transcendent mystery of a man's soul—
And it was more beautiful than I could bear.

In all the careers of humanity there must be no moment greater than that of knowing you were able to re-give life. And there must be no moment worse than that of knowing you tried, so hard, and lost. It is a rare person who is humble enough in the first . . . and brave enough in the second . . . to realize in both moments that he is not God.

With Manuelito, I saw Dr. Verdi's humility in the first moment. But with Riann Miles, I sensed Dr. Verdi's uncertainty in the second moment.

        I was in the middle of a parent-staff meeting on three-north when I felt a hand on my shoulder. I looked up, and Mrs. Cerci was motioning for me to come with her and her husband.

"We see Manuelito. First time. You come with. You pray."

All the blood in my body lumped in my stomach. It was another of those totally unexpected, beyond belief happenings that makes a job like chaplain worthwhile. I had thought that moment between Manuelito and his parents would have been the most private of private moments. I knew it was God and not "me" that they wanted in Intensive Care. But I knew, too, that they had understood my purpose.

The little boy was in the first bed to the left inside the door of Intensive Care. His head was wrapped in a gauze turban, and a large cake-carrier-shaped clear plastic steam hood was over his face and head.

He was asleep, but every now and then he made tiny whining, half-crying sounds. Vaseline was on his eyelids and eyelashes and the little multicolored blood pressure cuff was wrapped around his arm. He had several I.V. bottles and a urine catheter. There wasn't much swelling around his eyes, yet.

At first I stood back, dressed in the white sterile gown everyone entering Intensive Care must wear. Then they motioned for me to come closer. There really wasn't much we could do but stand there and be glad he was alive—and pray. And that's what we did.

        How inadequate it is to try to write about something like that.

17.

It was decided that Riann Miles would be given X-ray therapy. That's cobalt. The tumor—the one that could take fifteen years or so to grow big—was huge. Huge. Perhaps cobalt would stunt its growth, would stop it. Perhaps not.

Six weeks of treatments, five days a week. Sometimes cobalt makes you sick, nauseated. Your hair falls out. Six weeks. She'd stay in the hospital the whole time.

Riann was out of the three-north Constant Care room and back in a private room about five days after her craniotomy. She stayed in the hospital recuperating for about ten more days. Then she got to go home for a week. And then she came back for cobalt . . . six weeks.

It's difficult to describe Riann. Not only have I never met another child like her, I've never met another person like her. She is too good to be true.

Granted, it's easier to see only the good points in someone very ill. But that isn't the case with Riann. Anyone on three-north would agree; anyone who ever knew.

She is slender, like her mother, and has huge blue—clear blue —eyes and beautiful milk-white skin. She was eight when I first met her. And in the year I have known her, her face has matured, in moments here and there, to that of a wise woman. She is no longer a little girl. Yet her love is as innocent and trusting and complete as a little girl's.

During those six weeks of cobalt Riann enjoyed taking walks, often by herself, quietly, up and down the hospital corridors, looking. She would put on her pink quilted robe and dainty slippers and look much like the "lady of the house." But always quiet, always polite, never impatient.

The nurses would have parties in the small room behind the nursing station and they'd invite Riann. She was always so pleased, and somewhat awestruck, to be included in their fun. "Weren't they so nice to ask me?" she would say several times before being tucked into bed.

Saying prayers and tucking in became somewhat customary between Riann and me when her mother couldn't stay. She never counted on it, never asked to make me feel it was a duty. But if I was staying late, I could never feel the ends were tied until Riann had said her prayers and was tucked in.

It was during the time she was having cobalt treatments that I got to know her and her mother best. Six weeks is a long time.

Dr. Verdi had told the Mileses he thought they should get away for a week if they could, just the two of them. Mr. Miles still was having great difficulty accepting the *fact* of Riann's tumor. And Mrs. Miles was exhausted and under mounting pressure. So it was decided that they would see how Riann got along during her first two weeks of cobalt; and then, if that went well, they would go away the third week.

Cobalt wasn't something one could just do on another floor of Children's. To get to cobalt treatment Riann had to go by shuttle to Adult Hospital. Riann and her mother took me along one day during those first two weeks so I would know the procedure if I ever had to take Riann, which I had offered to do.

It was mid-March when the daily treks to Adult started. Riann would dress in the mornings, go to school for an hour—there was a school at Children's—then go to Adult for cobalt. And sometimes, if she felt all right, she and her mother would go out for lunch.

Riann would wear tights and shiny black patent shoes with straps and buckles, and little plaid skirts with matching solid-color sweaters and a furry-lined peacock blue parka with a hood. She always looked so cute dressed. I had seen her so much in night clothes.

Her mother taught her how to tie a scarf over her head and behind in a knot—right with the height of fashion, fortunately. She looked beautiful. You couldn't believe it.

Riann accepted everything—except shots and needles, and there were none with cobalt—and seemed to make a tiny adventure out of it.

The day I went with her and her mother "to cobalt" for the first time, she kept telling me about the slow elevator and the pictures on the wall and the small wooden playhouse in the therapy waiting room.

When I got there and saw the huge, ugly cobalt machine, I wondered how she remembered anything else. But she didn't even seem to notice. Or, if she did, she didn't say anything.

But that was the first time it went through me—the full impact —of how really sick Riann was . . . that one day she would be dead . . . one day, very likely, before her hair grew long.

The cobalt room was steely and barren. There was a huge metal table, above which hung the huge cobalt machine. Other than a small television monitor, there was virtually nothing else in the room.

Riann undressed almost completely and crawled up on the steel table. It dwarfed her. Then the technician lined up the cobalt machine with the red marks precisely painted on Riann's back and neck—red marks she wasn't allowed to wash off until all the cobalt treatments were over. Six weeks without a good bath.

Once that was done, we had to leave, all of us, even the technicians. Riann lay on her tummy, quiet and still . . . wearing only her white tights and her shiny black patent leather shoes. She looked so tiny and naked . . . and alone.

And she was.

In a few seconds it was over, she was dressed, and the three of us were on our way to lunch. Riann was doing better. The first week she had gotten nauseous four times. But so far this week she was fine. Her parents would be able to go away for a rest.

As Manuelito got better and better and returned from Intensive Care to his room on three-north, his mother felt more comfortable about leaving him for a few hours. One day she decided she wanted to see a "shop center."

I borrowed David's trusty Mercedes and took her to one. It was a riot. She had two other children, she said—Mary, who was five, and Anthony, who was four—and she was trying to buy clothing for them and for Manuelito.

The girl was bigger than most children her age, she explained, and the boy was smaller . . . and of course, *I* would know exactly what size Manuelito should have since I had seen him! (I have never bought clothing for a boy between the ages of one and sixteen years in my life!)

She also went wild at the costume jewelry counter and in the yard goods section. The salesladies were helpful and amused as we wandered about with our pocket dictionaries.

When we started the day I wasn't sure we'd be able to get through without lapsing into periods of great silence. But I don't think we stopped talking all day. It was fun!

But the Cercis were ready to leave when the time came. It had been a long haul.

The publicity department decided they would have a news conference to publicize the successful operation. Manuelito and his mother and father were to appear and Dr. Verdi would explain the surgical procedure and its effect.

And that news conference gave me an unplanned test of the validity of my decision to leave broadcasting.

I had told no one on three-north at University Children's about my broadcasting background. It wasn't that big a deal, but I didn't want it to influence anyone's thinking about me one way or the other. So consequently, only one or two people knew—by recognizing me—and they agreed not to say anything.

But I knew if I went to Manuelito's news conference, the jig would be up. I would know every one of the television reporters and cameramen . . . and they would know me.

I was anxious to see how I would react, what decision I would make when the time for the news conference came.

Mrs. Cerci had asked me to come to their room to help her dress Manuelito for the news conference and to say good-bye. They were going to leave right after, and I had to take Riann to cobalt, so that would be our only time for farewells.

Mrs. Cerci kept the door closed. The lady from P.R. fluttered in and out. At one time the conversation was so confusing that Mrs. Cerci thought for sure the P.R. lady wanted her to paste false hair on Manuelito's head for the television cameras!

Finally we had Manuelito dressed and their suitcases ready. I had noticed a large button that read, "Kiss Me, I'm Italian" in one suitcase. I laughed. Mrs. Cerci said Dr. Verdi had given that to Manuelito last week. I laughed again, but inside I flinched: Riann Miles had been so tickled when she had given that very same button to Dr. Verdi . . . I wondered why he gave it away. It bothered me.

The efficient P.R. lady knocked on the door. The press was waiting . . .

Mrs. Cerci scooped up Manuelito and thrust him into my arms for a good-bye hug. Then Mr. Cerci took him and they were ready.

"Come," Mrs. Cerci motioned to me.

"No, you go. It's for Manuelito and you, not me."

We hugged good-bye.

It was the last time I saw them.

The cameramen were all waiting at the corner of the hall. My ears were trained. When I heard the clicking and grinding stop and didn't see any more lights, I knew they had all disappeared down the hall to the conference room.

And not a bone in my body wanted to be on the other end of that story. They would write about a cute kid and a history-making operation. True.

But I saw the agony. I saw the real value of the reward.

No, I wouldn't have traded. The decision had been right. But then, I had never really doubted it in the first place.

The news conference for Manuelito was still going on when I left with Riann to go to cobalt. The little girl was all dressed and ready to go when I came to get her in her room. She had seen all the television people as they passed by the schoolroom door and had said good-bye to Manuelito that morning.

"He was so cute. Gee, I'll miss him. Mommy and I got him a little wooden toy at the gift shop last week. I gave it to him this morning. I hope he likes it. It was from all of us—Mommy and Daddy and Allison and Kevin and Eric and me."

"What about Silver Bullet and Gwennie and Marshmallow?" (one dog, two cats) I asked.

She giggled. "Oh yes, I forgot. Them too."

She was feeling good that day, thank goodness. The shuttle car was full, so she sat on my lap on the way. Strange emotions went through me, realizing I was holding a child so ill—terminally ill; a child I was beginning to love. Maybe that was the difference— the love. I still remember that ride vividly.

After cobalt we went to lunch at a restaurant near Children's. The food was good and they had old-time silent movies with music background. Riann loved it. She ordered shrimp—her favorite—and sat absolutely engrossed in the Laurel and Hardy film, giggling softly when something funny happened. She sat long after she had finished her shrimp. I figured she'd know when she was tired and wanted to go. She did; but not before she had eaten both our pickles—she is a pickle freak—and taken the Miller Beer coasters under our Cokes "for souvenirs."

If I were with a healthy child would I have remembered all those details? I doubt it. But now I had begun to grab at moments. I think we all did, all of us on three-north. Not each with the same child, but each with any child we began to love.

Except possibly for Dr. Verdi. Dying children, and loving them, still were two things he was wrestling with, or wrestling with admitting, even to himself. At least so it seemed to me.

He and Dr. Jenssen and I had lunch together a few days later. He still said he would give Riann fifteen years to live . . . Fifteen years . . . after seeing that massive tumor.

I think he suspected differently . . . knew differently . . . knew it couldn't be fifteen years. It just wouldn't come out of his mouth. His heart kept getting in the way.

Not only was Christian Verdi one of the best— if not *the* best—pediatric neurosurgeons in the world, he was ruggedly handsome, sensual and virile. He was in his mid-forties, looked a bit younger, drove a Maserati, wore Italian boots and custom-tailored cords, and Gucci—almost everything Gucci.

His hair was graying brown, long and full and wavy. He swaggered down the halls with authority and racy dignity. And he knew just what to say to a woman in a two-second passing to make her not quite sure he hadn't seduced her on the run.

Of course he was married.

One day he and I were discussing what it is like to be a chaplain; and what, on his part, it is like to work so hard for children such as Riann only to discover, in the end, that you can't get anywhere, that despite all the knowledge of medical science and all your surgical skill, the child ultimately will die.

During the conversation I sensed a despair in his voice, his difficulty as a surgeon to "let go," to accept that the child would die. And once he did let go, the difficulty of still relating to the yet living child as a human being with potential. I sensed that once he admitted defeat medically, the child was dead in his mind.

Maybe I was wrong. But I don't think so.

Dr. Verdi is not the type of man who can accept discussion of his possible weaknesses. He doesn't seem to have many. But he doesn't want others to see any at all. So I hesitated to give him "The Gift of the Dying Child" a few days later. But I finally did. I guess if there was to be a real working friendship, it couldn't be a "yes, sir" "yes, ma'am" one. It had to be one of concern, of mutual growing and respect.

THE GIFT OF THE DYING CHILD

She's not the same.
She's not the same!
    Her hair is shaved.
    Her head is cut.
    The tumor in her brain cannot come out.
She is dying.
    Oh God! She's not the same.
    She will never be the same again.

Look! She walks funny.
    Look. She doesn't walk at all.
Listen! Her memory is slipping.
    Listen. All is quiet.
    There is no more to remember.
She cannot see.
She cannot hear.
She cannot smile any more, doctor.
    She cannot even smile.

The tumor outran your cobalt.
The tumor outran your chemotherapy.
The tumor has outrun you, doctor.
    Or did you stop looking weeks ago?

She is not the same, her parents weep.
We did all we could, you say and hurry on.
There is nothing left. But to wait . . .
    Hurry up and die.
    Hurry up and die.
    We cannot stand it.
Oh dammit, God!—Why?
    Forget it. There is nothing more.
        Someday we will find a way.
        Someday our sick children will not die.

Quietly now, slip into her room, doctor.
    The sheets are white and crisp.

She is very pale.
She does not know you.
She will die before the next rounds.
Now take her hand that will not squeeze back,
And I will tell you what you missed.

You missed hearing good times remembered wistfully.
You missed easing the frustration of a thought
    Lost in midsentence, with a kiss.
You missed the time she gave her nurse
    A piece of rubber chocolate.
And the time she wore a big green button
    That read, "Bald is Beautiful!"
        And you couldn't cope with saving
        That simple moment of joy
        That came with the funny button she gave you . . .

You missed the waiting while she did things for herself
    As long as she could.
You missed the time she prayed
    That the tubes in her head would "shape up!"
You missed the times she prayed
    That *you* would have a "good night's sleep."
You missed kissing her good-night.
You missed kissing her at all . . .
    When she was not the same.

And so, doctor, you missed the gift of the dying child.

For if you will but share time—
    If you will but enjoy the dying child,
    She will teach you something more.
She will teach you to measure her life, and yours,
    Not only by their accomplishments,
    But by their gifts—
        Both those given and those received.

For the dying child will show you, if you but let her,

That the greatest gift
   Is not rewarded by acclaim,
   Does not hear the words "thank you,"
   Cannot see the smile of gratitude.
For the greatest gift is both given and received
WHEN YOU TRY TO LOVE WITHOUT CONDITION.
   When *you* can *do* no more,
   When you must set the dying child free—to die,
      Then it is hardest to love,
      For it is a love without condition.
      There is no reward to grasp.

But if it is here that you think you are farthest from God,
Then it is here that you are most mistaken.

For in learning to share this moment of time
   With the dying child,
You will learn to share in God's greatest gift to man:
   His unconditional love for us
   Despite his powerlessness
   In the face of our freedom to reject him.

If you can love the dying child, doctor,
   Despite your powerlessness
   In the face of her freedom to die—
      Then you cannot help but touch God.

      And your tears will fall on light,
      And you will have learned
      To share gifts with the dying child
         Beyond the diagnosis.

He said he liked it, understood its meaning. But I'm still not sure. He had told me he wanted to frame the writings I gave him about Manuelito. He never said the same about this.

It's walking a fine line to probe near a man's ego . . . especially a brilliant man at the top of his profession. They bruise more easily.

18.

Riann always loved to talk about her family. It was obviously a close, happy one.

"Why don't we write about your family?" I suggested one evening while her parents were on their week's "vacation." "We can take one person each night while your parents are away, and then put it all together in a big card for them when they return."

"You mean like a welcome home card?"

"Sure."

"Oh, that's a good idea! But I'm not too good at writing; could you do that?"

"OK. You just tell me things you like about each person, one person a night, and I'll write them down. Then I'll put it all on big sheets of colored paper and you can write 'Love, Riann' and the date at the bottom of each sheet."

"That's really a good idea. They'll be surprised!"

I knew what I was doing. So would Mrs. Miles . . . and maybe even Mr. Miles? It would be a bit difficult to take right then. But someday it would mean a lot.

For Riann, it was just a nice idea for a welcome home gift. That's all it should have been.

We had fun doing it. Each night before prayers I'd bring my brown notebook and pen into her room and we'd think—or she'd think.

"Oh, gee, what can I say," she'd ponder. Then she'd sit in deep concentration for a while. And then, sort of embarrassed, as if it wasn't very earthshaking, she'd come up with something she liked, or some incident she'd remember, about whoever in her family we were writing that night. "That really isn't very exciting," she'd apologize.

"It's not supposed to be exciting," I'd reassure her. "It's just supposed to be the things you remember and like about each person. It's called 'stream of consciousness.' "

"What?"

"Well, that's sort of saying the first thing that comes into your mind about someone. Those things usually are the things that impress you the most about a person."

"Oh, I see." She did, too. Her vocabulary and usage were excellent.

"You mean I said all that!" She was absolutely elated when I showed her the "welcome back" book in its final form.

"Sure you did."

"Gee, that's really nice. And I love the pictures," she giggled.

I had drawn some cartoon illustrations around the edges. Primitive, very.

I liked "Daddy's" and "Kevin's" pages best:

DADDY

When Daddy walks you can always hear him . . .
    In the morning coming down the hall . . .
    Because his shoes always make this funny sound,
    —Kind of "clump! clump!"

In the summertime
    When we don't have to go to school
    But Daddy has to go to work

When we wake up in the morning
We usually hear his car go
    Because his car makes this funny sound.

Sometimes at the dinner table
    When the boys act kind of funny and stuff,
    Daddy goes, "Cool it, cool down!"
And Allison and me,
    Sometimes we say, "Cool it, cool down,"
    To be funny.
When we do that, we usually stand up,
    And when we say, "Cool it,"
    We kind of bend our knees as we go down.

Sometimes when Daddy says
    He has to get a haircut
    I think it looks just right,
And I don't think he needs a haircut.

I think he's a nice Daddy.

                    Love, Riann . . . March 17th

KEVIN

Kevin is my brother.
    He is twelve years old.
He has a bike and sometimes rides it.
    But now since it's winter he doesn't.

Kevin has a dog named Silver Bullet.
    That's a funny name!
Silver Bullet is a basset hound,
    And he always wanders.

There's a dog up our street
    That he always goes to.
My father and Kevin usually

Have to go pick him up.
But he's a nice dog to have,
    Even though he wanders.

Whenever sometimes you pet Silver Bullet
    On his head . . .
It's like he has leftover fur on him.

Kevin has a girl friend,
    But we don't tease him about that.
He'll probably crush me for telling . . .

Sometimes Kevin is funny and tells jokes.
    He put my relics in the Seagram's bag.
Sometimes he calls me "Rube Tube"
    —Most of the time, anyway.
And I think that's a funny name!

                    Love, Riann . . . March 17th

Riann got out of bed three different times to
arrange the card "just so" for when her mother and father would
arrive . . . each time after someone had come in and looked
through it. She was so tickled.

"They'll bring a surprise for me, I'm sure," she said. "And now
I'll have a surprise for them!"

Saying prayers with Riann was difficult at times
—for me. It was her frankness and her sense of humor, and her
acceptance.

Granted, the words "tumor," and "tubes" (shunts) likely
didn't have the same connotation for her as they did for me. But
hearing her use them so freely in open conversation with God
made me cold.

The ritual was always the same. First we'd get out the blue
velveteen Seagram's bag that held several religious "relics." She

would choose two, usually . . . or maybe three. Often she would comment, "This is my favorite," or, "Grandmother sent me this one; it has a real piece of the Cross in it."

Then we would each choose a printed prayer to read. Her favorite was "Courage."

And then we'd begin. She always wanted me to start. So I would read the prayer I had chosen, then say one extemporaneously.

And then she would pray . . .

COURAGE

God make me brave,
  Let me strengthen after pain,
As a tree strengthens after the rain,
  Shining and lovely again.

As the blown grass lifts,
  Let me rise from sorrow
With quiet eyes,
  Knowing Thy way is wise.

God make me brave,
  Life brings such blinding things,
Help me to keep my sight,
  Help me to see aright,
That out of dark comes light.

And then she would continue on her own. "Dear God, I hope Mommy has a good sleep and Daddy has a good sleep and Allison and Kevin and Eric and Dr. Verdi and Dr. Jenssen and Nina and all the other doctors and nurses have a good sleep . . . and all the children in the hospital, too. And Bullet and Gwennie and Marshmallow . . .

"Thank you for a nice day. Thank you that I didn't get sick after cobalt. That's ten days in a row!

"Please don't let my tumor get bigger. Please don't let me have any more headaches. And please tell the tubes in my head to shape up!

"Please let tomorrow be as nice as today."

Then she would look up at me to let me know she had finished, so we could say the "Our Father" together. As I mentioned earlier, I still haven't been able to say the Lord's Prayer once without thinking of Riann, without hearing her bell-like voice praying along with me. Maybe if I tried hard not to remember, I could. Maybe I want to remember. Maybe sharing the memory gives a deeper meaning to the prayer.

Soon the last day of cobalt treatments was drawing near. "I can take a bath! I really can hardly wait. A real bath!" said Riann anxiously.

Riann was growing tired of the cobalt treatments. And though she didn't complain too much, we could tell that having all of the little hair she had left fall out in clumps by its roots was getting to her.

Yet, still she was beautiful.

Her last cobalt treatment was to be on Friday and she was to go home Saturday morning. Everyone on three-north who knew Riann was happy for her. She had spent most of the winter in the hospital, and now, soon, she'd be free to go home. The beginning of the "grace period."

On three-north we all knew she'd be back, be a patient again, likely die here.

But when? How long? How much suffering? They're the horrible unanswered questions; the questions of each day, every day. The waiting for the other shoe to drop.

19.

In the little hospital in a small town in the southern tip of the state that same Saturday that Riann went home to Rock Shores they were telling Ken Harrington that he had two choices. That his baby being born at that moment had such a large head that the doctors either could crush the head and let the baby be born naturally—but dead; or that they could do a Caesarean section and try to save the baby. But either way, they were sure the baby was severely deformed.

What could the poor man do? He said Caesarean section. It takes time to decide that "killing" your own baby may be best.

I took one look at Lisa Harrington as she was raced down the three-north hall in an incubator several hours later and I knew her diagnosis immediately: acute hydrocephalus.

Her head was immense; and when I looked closer, I saw that both her feet were bent inward—clubbed. But it was her head, so very very big.

"You'd better stay around, Rev." It was Patrick McMahan. "She may go soon. But come to think of it," he added, "the mother is still in the hospital and the father had to go back with the ambulance, so I guess you'd just be staying around for the kid, if you stay . . ."

"Oh, stay." It was Dr. Gary Suter. "I'm almost out of cigarettes!" He looked at my nearly full pack. (It's nice to be needed.) "We'll do an angiogram to see if there's much brain, and then we'll put in a shunt," said Dr. Suter.

I went along to angio. Dr. McMahan had a terrible time finding the arteries. Then, right in the middle of the procedure, the baby started not doing too well. "She may not get through this," said Dr. McMahan.

"I wonder if she's been baptized?" I asked. "If she's Catholic it may make a difference."

"You're right, Rev. Let's try to find out. That's important." Patrick McMahan is Catholic.

The word came back. The baby wasn't baptized, but there was no way, right then, to determine her religion.

"Go ahead, Rev. It can't hurt," said Dr. McMahan, who was still trying to find the second artery.

"OK." I was very nervous. I had never baptized a child before. I knew it was legal in an emergency, with the Catholic Church, I mean; but my knees still shook.

I didn't have much time to think, though. It had to be done quickly. We got a small paper lab cup. Patrick McMahan and I stood on either side of the baby . . . the baby whose head was held, tilted backwards, between two sponge rubber padded braces; the baby in whose neck was one needle piercing the artery; the baby who was lying bundled on a steel table under a massive X-ray machine . . . and I poured water on her forehead and said, "I baptize you in the name of the Father and of the Son and of the Holy Spirit, Amen. May the Lord bless you and keep you and make his face shine upon you, now and forevermore, Amen."

I kissed her. So did Dr. McMahan. Then Gary Suter lit a cigarette and "charted" the baptism and Dr. McMahan found the other artery and I watched. My knees still felt funny.

The dye didn't go anywhere. It just stopped. Lisa Harrington had virtually no brain.

In the complete, normal angiogram series, the dye looks like branches of a tree in the X-ray, with two main branches and lots of little continuous branches reaching and spreading from the front to the back of the head. But in Lisa Harrington's head, the dye just stopped. There were no spreading branches on the X-rays. Just two main branches. Then virtually nothing, virtually no brain system.

"I opt for no shunt," said Patrick McMahan. "It's useless. It's cruel. Why make her suffer more? She's going to die. She has no brain system."

"I agree, tonight at least," said Gary Suter, who was senior to Patrick McMahan. "C.B. [Dr. Verdi] will have the final say, though, you know."

"Yeah, I know."

It wasn't a matter of disagreement, really, between Dr. McMahan and Dr. Verdi. Because really there is no right or wrong. But the problem is a matter of growing concern: when to treat and when not to treat when you *know* the patient will die anyway.

The doctor in the small downstate hospital had left the decision at birth to the father. But in all fairness, did either of them have time to act beyond instinct in the crisis situation? And, in almost all cases, instinct tells us, as human beings, to preserve life.

Perhaps the child's hydrocephalus could have been controlled. Perhaps she would have had a healthy body and complete brain and intercranial system. That wasn't known for sure as she was pushing to get out of her mother's womb.

But now it was known. How much should the physician "treat" now? How many medical procedures should be performed now . . . when it was simply prolonging death rather than preserving life?

Dr. Verdi ordered a shunt for Lisa Harrington. So rather than a small basketball, her head soon began to look like a large prune. Orthopedic doctors put tiny casts on both of Lisa Harrington's legs and feet, and they put stiff moldings around her hands to try to straighten her bent fingers.

And the nurses moved her away from the window . . . so people walking by in the corridor wouldn't stare and point.

It may have hurt Lisa Harrington when each of these procedures happened to her. Under the circumstances, it could be asked, "Weren't these heroic means? Was it necessary? Couldn't she be allowed to die in peace, without surgery, without casts, without moldings . . . just be fed and held and let die in peace?"

What is life anyway? Does it end when the heart stops beating
. . . when the brain doesn't function . . . or when a person is
rendered incapable of both giving and receiving love?

I've never been sure why the doctors did all that to—or for—
Lisa Harrington. They seem to go in spurts. At times they use
"heroic" means for a newborn who they know will die. But for
an older child in the last stages of dying of a brain tumor, they
will mercifully, quietly, "open the window and close the door,"
will not use heroic means.

But then, in each case, the doctors have had their day, their
chance. They have *made the attempt to save life*, whether it be
for the newborn or the older child. I guess when you're a surgeon,
when saving life is what you breathe to do, you cannot do other-
wise: Start out to save, despite the odds. End up quietly opening
the window and letting the child go free . . . to die.

I dread the coming day when breast-beating moralists will
engage in public uproar over the agonized life-death decisions
made by concerned physicians in the quiet corridors of this na-
tion's hospitals. The decisions are made every day—decisions to
treat, decisions not to treat, decisions to use heroic means, decisions to pull the plug. But until I have to make one myself, I don't
intend to write a rule book.

         Lisa Harrington was ultimately taken to a nursing
home where she died about a month later. She was Catholic. Her
father cried in relief about the baptism.

Alex Felini was still unconscious. They took him to surgery three more times after the day we prayed and cried in the chapel. But it hadn't helped.

One Saturday—my last official Saturday at Children's—Alex stopped breathing. He was in room 383, a small, private room next to the Constant Care room on three-north. He had been there about a month. His head was bandaged and the CFS tube stuck out. He also had two I.V.s. He was still decerebrate. His eyes were open now, but they didn't react to light or move.

We didn't know if he could hear us or not. But we would talk to him, all of us. We'd tell him hospital news and funny things that the doctors and nurses did. His parents talked to him. About what was going on at home, about his sisters, Chrissy and Sandi, about horses and cars and baseball and horses and horses.

His father even made a cassette tape recording of each member of the family talking and asked the nurses to play it now and again when he and his wife couldn't be there.

Sometimes we'd believe Alex moved. Sometimes we'd believe we heard him make a sound. Maybe he did.

We would dream about him . . . waking up, sitting up, talking, running down the halls with his six-shooters, saying "Quack, Quack, I'm a duck"—one of his favorite imitations.

But they were only dreams. And that Saturday he stopped breathing.

I was sitting at the end of the hall in the small waiting room. I saw Tony Felini walk by to visit Alex. He was in a good mood. He stopped and chatted for a minute, then went on toward 383.

About three minutes later, an agonizing scream came from the other end of the hall. No actor could duplicate it. It told a story without words.

Tony Felini came running out of room 383, screaming. "Oh God! Oh no! Alex, Alex! No! No! No! Oh God! Don't let him die! Alex, *don't* die! Alex don't die!"

"Code 1111—three-north, room 383. Code 1111—three-north, room 383. Code 1111—three-north, room 383. Code 1111 —three-north, room 383."

Some hospitals are more subtle. They'll page Dr. Sam Smith, or Dr. Red, when they really mean "emergency." But it's all the same. People figure it out. You don't have to be around Children's long to realize that "Code 1111" is red alert—pull out all the stops, drop what you're doing, run—someone has stopped breathing.

Medical staff came out of the woodwork. The neurosurgeons, who had finished rounds only fifteen minutes earlier, came up the back stairway in a pack.

But no one could go near Tony Felini. He had run out of Alex's room and was standing in the middle of the nursing station flailing his arms and screaming. No one dared too near. If anyone had tried to talk with him, calm him down, he wouldn't have heard.

"Can you just stay with him," I was asked as the nurses ran back and forth.

"Sure," I said. But there was nothing to do but stand and watch. Even a strong man could have done nothing.

There's a large metal refrigerator on three-north by the nursing station. Tony Felini started beating his fists against it. His eyes were wild, his face damp and white.

He had nowhere to run.

He started beating his head against a wall.

"Neen"—Carrie Felini was the only person I had ever found who could shorten Nina—"Is he gone?"

Alex's petite, dark-haired mother stood by the nursing station divider wall . . . quiet, composed. Just one simple question.

She had been in the coffee shop when the "Code 1111" came. She recognized it.

"I don't know, Carrie."

"No." It was Mary Cooke. "He's OK, Mrs. Felini. He just stopped breathing for a few seconds. But he's OK now."

"Thanks, Mar."

"He's OK, Mr. Felini," Mary repeated to Alex's father. "He's OK. He's breathing fine again. Why don't you sit down? Go in the back room. He's fine. You can see him in a few minutes."

Somehow, Tony Felini dragged himself to the back room. He sat very still . . . unseeing, unhearing . . . just sitting, staring. "Alex, you can't die. Come on, Alex. Come on Alex. Don't die. God, please don't let him die. I've prayed so hard. Come on kid. I love you." The words came out in metered time, quietly, like an echo. "I love you . . ."

"You know, Neen, I guess I'm selfish, but I wanted it to be over. I wanted him to die, now. If he's not gonna get better, ever, I mean. *If he's gonna get better, I'll wait any of them out.* But if he's not, why let him lie there like that, day in and day out?"

Carrie Felini was still standing by the nursing station entrance. Tony Felini was still sitting in the back room. I was going back and forth. The doctors and nurses were still in with Alex.

"And all my friends and relatives," Carrie went on, "they mean well, don't get me wrong, but every day it's the same thing. They think they have to call. And then they ask the same questions, every day: 'How's Alex? Any change? What about his temperature? What about his blood pressure? What about his brain swelling? Are his eyes still dilated? Does he seem to be more aware?'

"If something has gotten worse, they don't seem to hear it. If something has gotten better, they try to latch onto it, to build me up—to build themselves up. I just wish they'd let me alone. If there's any dramatic change, I'll let them know. But nothing changes, day after day, week after week. I'd not answer the phone, but I'm always afraid it's the hospital.

"Tony can't take it, either. I think Alex is going to die. I really do. I think a lot of people around here are beginning to think so, too. But Tony doesn't. Tony still expects Alex to wake up and say, 'Hi, Dad! Hi, Mom!'"

"Neen, I can't even hold Alex . . . with all those tubes and things. I just want to hold him. He's my little boy, my only boy. I'm his mother. I just want to hold him. But maybe it's best after all, that I can't hold him . . . with him this way, because he wouldn't respond, wouldn't hug back . . . and that would be worst of all."

I agreed with her then. I was beginning to think Alex would die, too. So, I think, was Dr. Praeder.

But even realistic Patrick McMahan wasn't one hundred percent sure. There still was that thread . . .

21.

Riann Miles had a good summer, really good. Her father had wanted to take the family on a ranch/riding/camping-out vacation in the west. I can remember thinking it was a pipe dream as he talked about it the day of her surgery.

But they went, all of them. And Riann made it. She was so happy "just to have made it!" On their Christmas card of family pictures that year there was one of Riann standing in front of a tent holding a roll of bathroom tissue. It was a comment on her most difficult problem of the trip—how to crouch when what your brain tumor is doing to your body won't really let you crouch comfortably.

But it was a comment on the whole rotten deal, too.

The good summer turned into a relatively good fall. Riann went back to school—not whole days every day, but as much as possible.

Her classmates accepted her situation and, thanks to a perceptive, kind teacher, very likely learned a great deal from it.

I saw Riann in her home once before the camping trip and twice in the fall. It isn't difficult to visit Riann. She is always happy. She talks about her trip west and about school . . . and about University Children's. Her memories of the hospital and people there are quite vivid, and always positive . . . except for the needles.

Riann seems to have reached a plateau. Other than a slight limp, she can walk well. She can't run and play hard and she tires easily, and her memory doesn't always work at one hundred percent in momentary things. But other than that, she seems not to be getting any worse.

"I have so many things going on inside me. I'm so *glad* she's doing well . . . but each morning I wake up and think—before I even get my eyes open—will *this* be the day? Will today be the one that she changes, that she starts going downhill? Will she suddenly be dead in her bed one morning? Each time she gets a headache I ask, 'Is this it, God? Is this one it?' If she has an upset stomach or throws up, I ask, 'Is it the tumor, or the shunt . . . or does she just have indigestion, or a flu-bug, like a normal eight-year-old?' " It was Mrs. Miles on the telephone one early fall evening.

"I try to tell myself to live each day at a time, but it's not always easy. And Eric [her husband] think's she's fine. He'll hardly even talk about it. Ever since she made it through that trip west, he's sure she'll be fine for years.

"You know, when we had been on horseback for hours and finally got to the campground where we were going and Riann and I were alone unpacking some things, she started to cry. I was sure she was sick. I was so frightened.

" 'No, Mommy, I'm all right,' she told me. 'I'm just crying because I'm so happy. I'm so happy I made it . . . like everybody else.'

"I guess it was good for her. But that almost broke me in two. She was so brave . . . so brave. God! A brain tumor, two major surgeries—craniotomies—and riding horseback up some mountain. She could be dead next year at this time . . .

"Sometimes people say it's better if a child goes quickly. Others say we're lucky to have this time. I'm *glad* we have the time . . . but the uncertainty, the not knowing, the raw fear gets to me after a while. I worry about Eric, too. I don't want him to feel guilty about anything . . . when it's over. That's why I was *so* glad this trip went well. If something had gone wrong . . . with Riann . . . he may have felt guilty for years."

Guilt: That's the one major feeling parents have, I was finding out, that Elisabeth Kübler-Ross's patients didn't have. The sixth point. Yes, parents have the famous five: disbelief (shock), anger, bargaining, despair, and acceptance. They usually begin with disbelief—almost always; rarely end with acceptance simultaneous with or preceding death; and go through the other three in no particular order and often with one overlapping the other.

But guilt . . . With parents of critically and terminally ill children, it's a major point.

Guilt takes several shapes in this context. "I didn't get my child to a doctor fast enough." "I did something (took something, ate something, didn't do something) during pregnancy that caused my child to have a birth defect." "I haven't bought my child the things I should have." "I haven't loved my child enough." "I haven't really gotten to know my child." "Why didn't I take him to the fair?" "Why didn't I give him . . ." It goes on and on. And it's very, very real.

In my opinion, this guilt has to be affirmed—affirmed as normal. So often I'll hear a doctor or a nurse or a friend say, "Oh, you shouldn't feel guilty." If they're medical people answering a medical-genetic question, fine. But even then I think the answer should be preceded by, "Most parents ask the same questions, have the same guilty feelings; it's normal. But in your case, as in most cases, it is completely unfounded . . ." And then continue with their medical-genetic explanation.

But for other types of guilt, the more parents are told, "Don't talk that way; you have no reason to feel guilty; you shouldn't say that; you shouldn't feel that," the more they will suppress their true feelings and begin to imagine they're abnormal, or even losing their minds.

I have found it is much better to say, "I can see why you would say that . . . why you would feel that way. Johnny's situation was so unexpected . . . and your reaction is quite normal." Then make a transference to myself. "If my parents were to become very ill suddenly, or die—and they live in Maryland—I'm sure I would feel very guilty. I'd chastise myself for not going home more often, or writing or telephoning more often, or not being kinder . . . It's a normal reaction.

"But in your case, you have a choice. Are you going to let those natural guilt feelings overwhelm you and so engulf you that you neglect Johnny, who really needs you now . . . or neglect the rest of your family? Or, are you going to admit that the guilt feelings are normal—accept them—and let them subside naturally while you get on to more important things, like loving Johnny and sharing with him and appreciating him . . . or helping bring your whole family closer together in this important time? It's your choice. Nobody can make it for you."

I talked with Mrs. Miles about guilt on the telephone that evening. And how they were lucky to have borrowed time . . . but how difficult it was not to know . . . to wait . . . for what?

Then I wrote again . . . about three in the morning . . . a prayer
for Mrs. Miles to pray . . .

A Prayer to Read in Winter

One summer, I asked.
  You could have seen snow
On broad green maple leaves, and known
  That the warmth of April was best.

But no, my little one
  Wanted to pick daisies and catch fireflies.
So she melted waiting icicles with life's warm breath
  —she and You.
You work well together!

I live with hours; yet my heart dares to see
  Daisies in December.
But it *will* snow someday. And flakes
  Will blanket tiny petals and fool the sun.
For seasons live and die—and live again.
  Like God. Like man.

But, God, don't let me, shivering,
  Miss the gift of winter,
Whose frigid eyes now pierce me through
  With each morning's first breath.

For in stillness winter whispers,
  "There is a secret. There is a secret.
Life will burst onto the face of the Earth,
  And leftover ice drip from daisies,
    And you will call it spring.
But life is *made* while you wait on frozen soil."

One summer, I asked. It is a gift glorious!
  But when winter comes, my little one will *know its secret*
    —of life, of love, of rebirth,

And winter will be *her* gift glorious.
  For she will see Your face; while I still wait and dream
  And cry on naked branches.

Oh God! Don't let me be so frail at losing my gift,
  That I fail to share the joy of hers.

That was for Mrs. Miles.

But I wrote some things for Riann, too. It started innocently
with a short little story about "Ferd S. Soap"—the bar of soap she
used for her "first bath" after cobalt . . . Went on to a horse
named "Bruce"—supposedly the horse she would ride on her trip
west . . . included a bluebird named Homer and a frustrated
turkey named Thomas . . . And ended up with Clive Thurgood
Bookworm, III, who was destined to become the subject of several
stories, and Riann's favorite. Luckily, I found a red, orange, and
yellow stuffed bookworm at a local department store and sent it
to Riann. She carried him around with her for her remaining
time.

He watched her die.
For in the interim of my writing, that has happened.

The first false alarm with Riann came at Thanks-
giving. Like false labor pains in reverse. But she was all right, in
and out of the hospital overnight. She had started to throw up,
and had had a headache Friday morning after Thanksgiving. But
apparently one of her shunts had just clogged temporarily. Whatever it was, she went home again Saturday afternoon.
Home for Christmas.
It was a pretty winter day, the day I visited Riann just before
Christmas. I had borrowed David's Mercedes and I played Christmas tapes on the stereo all the way to Rock Shores.

When I arrived, Mrs. Miles was "at the grocery and would be right back." The day housekeeper was there with Riann.

One of my best memories of Riann is as she half-skipped, half-walked, half-limped out through the dining room to meet me. She had on blue slacks and a white turtleneck shirt, and it was the first time she wasn't wearing a scarf over her head.

"Riann! Look at your hair! All that hair! That's fantastic! I can't believe it!"

She grinned from ear to ear, and giggled and giggled. She was so happy, so very, very happy. Her hair must have been one-quarter inch long all over.

She gave me a "big hug" (as her mother always called it) and a kiss on the lips.

Her right arm and hand were getting weaker each time I saw her. And the Christmas package I had for her was rather large. But when I held it up for her to see, that it was for her, she sort of reached for it.

I gritted my teeth and put it in her arms. And she managed! It was an immense effort, but she managed!

"I started to cry in the middle of the supermarket. All the people and the 'Merry Christmas' and the fruits and candies and goodies . . . all the smells . . . and playing Christmas carols over the loudspeaker.

"People must have thought I was crazy. I couldn't help it. I just started to cry, and I had to leave," Riann's mother whispered to me a few minutes after she came home.

The three of us had lunch and talked about Christmas and Santa, and about what Riann wanted, and about traditions and turkeys, and how her ninth birthday was just too close to Christmas—"only two days after!"

Then Riann, grumbling as all children do who must take afternoon naps, went upstairs to rest.

"I just want it to be over—Christmas. I know that's awful. But I do. How can I be happy? I keep saying, 'It will be our last Christmas together.' And it will. Even Dr. Verdi admits that now. He says six months at best . . . probably less. Six months!"

"And Eric *still* doesn't seem to see. He still goes to meetings, meetings, meetings every evening."

Escape? Denial? I suggest.

"Yes, I guess it is his way of denying, his way of escaping the truth. But I don't want him to have regrets later . . .

"Last night I told him if he wants his family to be together after this—after all this—he'd better stay at home from now on. No more night committee meetings. He'll have years for that. I just can't carry all this by myself. I just can't. I need him.

"I can't be cheerful for Riann and answer the other children's questions—and they're beginning to figure this out; they'll have to be told the truth soon, just like Dr. Verdi said, we would know when they are ready—and keep house, and talk to relatives and friends, and be a wife, too. It's not fair."

(It wasn't. But it was normal, too. Men—at least the men I observed—seem to have greater difficulty accepting abnormalities of any kind in their children. Be it an assault on their maleness, or an unusually squeamish stomach by gender, or an inability to deal with interruptions in the normal order of things, or a prolonged state of shock, as it was for Mr. Miles. Any or all of them. These men couldn't accept the *fact* of sick or dying children as well as women . . . couldn't deal with their feelings about them as openly. And I think that's true of men—fathers—as a whole. Usually they just pack it away inside, layer on layer. And consequently, the statistics of broken marriages in this area are high.)

We talked an hour more in the den as the sun slipped behind the trees.

"I read it. I read the whole book!" Riann walked hesitantly

down the stairs in her heavy brown laced shoes. "It really was a nice book. Thank you."

As one of her Christmas gifts I had given her a copy of *Big Susan*, my absolute favorite child's Christmas book, about doll-house dolls who come alive each Christmas eve.

We talked and laughed some more, and a light snow began to fall. Oh, if only it had been a normal happy Christmas visit. No hanging sword. No dangling shoe . . .

She stood shivering. "I'm glad when you come. I can always get all that stuff out. It does me good."

I stuck the key in the frozen cardoor lock. "Riann's so happy. She's almost blissfully happy." And she was. "And that's the most important thing right now," I said.

"You're right, you're really right. Thank God for that! I'll just have to keep reminding myself of that, I guess. Over and over. And you are right, she *is* happy. I can't believe it. And it *is* the most important thing now. I have tons of tomorrows to cry . . . Merry Christmas."

"Merry Christmas."

I drove down the driveway, waving.

Bah! Humbug!

22.

Alex Felini didn't have a good summer . . . from our human perspective. He died.

When I came back to three-north to visit that summer I always visited Alex, too. He had been moved from room 383, the small, private room, to a four-bed room. But it didn't make any difference. He lay there, getting thinner and thinner and looking less and less like six-gun Alex, and never regaining consciousness.

But his father kept talking to him.

His mother kept talking, too . . . about other things, to people other than Alex, laughing and joking and going on living. But she talked less and less *about* Alex. For there was less and less to talk about. There were no more questions. It was more than a coma; more than brain swelling. He was going to die.

He remained decerebrate; he developed an infection; and his pupils dilated—the worst sign. "Whether" one day turned quietly to "when," and I could have prayed Carrie's prayer.

A "no code" was ordered. No more "Code 1111" if Alex stopped breathing, no heroic means, no more torture. It wouldn't be preserving life, it would be prolonging death.

"Hi, Nina! Hey, Alex, Nina's here. Man, you should see the tan she has. You better get well fast so you can get a tan, too. The summer's almost over.

"Nina's working for a lawyer now, and she's also working part-time as a chaplain at North Side Hospital."

(When I had to leave Children's in June because the new students were coming, Paul had given me a job, and I had volunteered to help the chaplain at North Side, near my home, in the evenings.)

"You remember North Side," Tony Felini went on, "where Mommy's doctor is. Yeah, Alex, Neen's got a real good tan."

Alex lay there, eyes open in a blank stare. Huge, huge eyes, now, against his hollow gray-white face.

"Hi, Alex," I said. "If you think my tan's good, you should see Jennifer's! She loafs around all day in the sun." I went along. It would have been cruel not to. He knew; Tony Felini knew. But he had played the game so long now he didn't know how to change, didn't want to "give up" in public. As if giving up in public would have "killed" Alex. But it was a superstition not teased by hope this time around.

"Hey, Neen, I was thinking," Tony Felini turned to me. "They've got a chapel at North Side, don't they?"

"Yes."

"Well, we've been bringing all these St. Jude candles for Alex, as you know . . ." High-strung laughter. "Well, we've still got all the empty glass jars—you know, after the candles have been burned up. Well, I kind of hate to just throw them away. I figure somebody somewhere could use them. For a while I just put them on the chapel desk downstairs, but then I seen them in the wastebasket. If I'd wanted them there, I could've done that my-self . . .

"So, anyway, I was wondering if you'd like them to use at North Side?"

"Sure. I'm sure there are people there who would appreciate them." At the moment, I wasn't certain what I'd do with empty St. Jude candle jars. But of course, that wasn't the point. Those jars were wrapped up in the mystery of Alex's life and death. Tony Felini didn't want to see them in a wastebasket, not yet.

I guess I didn't either. Sometimes it's hard for gut reaction to travel to intellectual realism and acceptance.

"Well, I tell you what—now, these are all empty, you know—"

"Sure."

"Well, I'll drop them off at North Side some day next week on the way out here to see Alex. Do you have an office there?"

I explained how to get to the chaplain's office at North Side and told him to leave them on the desk if I wasn't there.
That was Thursday.

Alex died Saturday morning . . . two days later.

Three nurses from three-north and I went to the funeral Monday morning. It was an open casket. Alex was wearing a red plaid sports jacket and beside him was a plastic horse. That was the most real thing of all . . . the plastic horse.

I remember seeing Tony Felini sitting not more than three feet away from Alex's head, staring. He didn't see anything or anybody but Alex. The rims of his eyes—like the eyes of Ethel Stone's father so many months earlier—were like blood. His skin was translucent green. And when the lid of the casket was closed and snapped into place, his one solitary moan was beyond my experience to comprehend.

Another thing affected me, too, that August morning. It was the nurses, the fact that they came. One was Jennifer Bradford. The other two, Mary Katharine Soloman and Karen Greer, worked the overnight shift. I barely knew them. They all loved Alex a lot.

A few days later I put my feelings into words, but then I just put the pages away. It was too soon to show it to them. Maybe I would some day.

THREE-NORTH

The sun was blazing in the east window of the nursing station and the shifts were changing from night to day when Alex died.

The shifts kept changing and the sun crawled up over the roof and down the other side and around and up again, as is its mission.

On its third trip, Alex was buried.

In a room that always wears soft orange lamps that look like vases, always wears the smell of flowers, always wears the silence of sick tension, stood three girls. Not everyone recognized them as they walked by the open casket. They were not "in place" without their nursing uniforms of white or pales of yellow, pink, or blue.

Alex was not "in place" either. He wasn't running up and down the hospital corridors going, "Quack, quack, I'm a duck!" or "Bang, bang, you're dead!" He wasn't playing "General Custard" with his ever-present plastic horses.

He wasn't trying to postpone the moment of medicine by saying, "Wait a minute, nurse; let's discuss this whole thing!" or "Wait a minute, nurse; I've just gotta go to the john! Things like that can't wait, you know."

Neither Alex nor the three nurses were "in place."
No one had told Alex he would die without waking to see summer.

No one had told the nurses their jobs would make their hearts take them to the funerals of seven-year-old children.

I have watched these nurses, and all the neurosurgical nurses on three-north at University Children's, give greater human meaning to their profession than most people could imagine; than even they themselves would likely imagine.

I have watched their nursing care remain professional. But I have watched their faces tighten and their words get scarce as they see a child they have grown to love hooked onto a respirator, or diagnosed "malignant brain tumor," or lapse into uncontrollable seizures . . . or die.

I have watched them sit for a moment in the nursing station, trying to be unobtrusive as they hold their stomachs or clench their fists, knowing they have to go into the room of a child who has been through surgery and give him a shot that will hurt him *one more time* and make him cry. When all they want to do is love him and hold him and comfort him and make him happy.

I have watched them cry in a corner behind a curtain when

a brave father whose baby suddenly died walked to a surgeon, shook his hand, and said, "Thank you, doctor, I know you did everything you could."

I have watched them grab any available moments to comfort a frightened child, or give cuddling and love to a newborn, or talk with worried parents.

And in the midst of the daily pain of three-north, I have watched these nurses make joy. I have watched them use their own money to buy clothes and toys for a sick and abandoned newborn, and have small parties whenever there is the most fragile excuse to celebrate. I have watched them grasp these moments of joy and hold fast . . .

In a few short months at Children's, I have watched all this. And I have developed a deep respect for these nurses for the *caring* in their care, and for the reflection of a Greater Love that shines through them on their patients, on each other, and on their profession.

For after all, no one told them their jobs would make their hearts take them to the funerals of seven-year-old children. They went, and will continue to go, because for them the word "nurse" means love, too.

Unlike Riann's parents, Alex's had no period of "borrowed time." By the time the "whether" turned to "when" there was no more breathing time, no responsive child. The other shoe had dropped, and the waiting was only for it to settle.

That same Monday evening after Alex's funeral I went to North Side Hospital. I usually arrived after the staff chaplain had gone, and this was the case that evening.

I got out my keys to the office, unlocked the door, and flicked on the light. On the chaplain's desk I saw a large brown paper bag. My name was written on the side.

I put down my purse and keys and opened the bag. Inside were seven St. Jude candles . . . four empty, and three still unburned. The accompanying note read: "To Nina, from Alex Felini."

I sat in that office a long time. It was the brown paper bag that got me immediately. The comparison between the brown paper bag of seven months earlier . . . the one that held Ethel Stone's furry pink coat . . . and this brown paper bag, which held said and unsaid prayers for Alex Felini's life.

But there was more. Was Tony Felini saying, in Alex's name, "Here, take your damned St. Jude candles . . . for all the good they did me! Look, three of them aren't even burned. Thanks, God. Thanks a lot. Thanks for nothing."

And if Tony Felini wasn't saying that on that Monday evening . . . was I?

About six weeks later, after all the autopsy results were in, it was determined that Alex Felini had an inoperable, undetectable brain tumor. That, and not the posterior fossa cyst, had caused his death.

At least there was a reason. People with posterior fossa cysts aren't expected to die. People with inoperable brain tumors oftentimes are expected to die.

That made it all all right, of course.

23.

I was coming out of my shell shock. Very slowly, very painfully, I was beginning to try to add one and one . . . add God and pain . . . and come up with a solution. I knew all along it was impossible. No one had to tell me there is no answer to the "problem" of pain and death. But now, in the winter of Riann Miles's life . . . in the winter after Alex Felini's death, I was beginning to want to think about it. I was beginning to want to wrestle with the "mystery"—aiming for an answer, but knowing that I would settle for a rationalization, a seeing "through a glass darkly."

I began to read, to see what others had thought on the mystery of suffering. Many theologians and philosophers chose to approach suffering and death as a "problem" rather than as a "mystery." Some wrestled with whether we were created good and went downhill from there, or whether we were created with holes —immature—and given the potential to lift ourselves up by our bootstraps. Many others compared pain with goodness as they compared hot water with cold: In other words, if there isn't pain with which to compare happiness (goodness, love, etc.), how can we know that we are happy?

Others spent a great amount of time discussing what happens when we die: the pan-cosmic nature of the separated soul; our total personhood achieved; our eternal "yes" or "no" to God. And still others wrote off the reason, the "origin" of pain in deference to dealing with the cleansing "purpose," the transforming power of pain. (Almost everyone I read had done this one.)

At the time the events of this chapter happened I hadn't read all these theories yet. I couldn't have coped with all of them then, not and had them make much sense. But I was beginning.

It was strange to be reading about pain and death as a theological-philosophical "problem" or "mystery." I would get angry and disagree. Or, I would stop at one sentence or paragraph that made some sense to me and then spend half an hour mentally applying it, reliving experiences, testing its validity in my own experience, and either building on it or discarding it as invalid for me. I didn't always get very far in reading numbers of pages that way, but I did get far in exercising my mind, in wrestling with *my* most relevant mystery about God—the mystery of pain and evil. There were still a lot of apples and oranges. But the potential for a jelly of sorts was there.

No great or small theologian I stumbled across told me why there is a world, answered the mystery of creation and history. An anthropologist and naturalist, Dr. Loren Eiseley, told me where I probably came from—a rather ugly Crossopterygian affectionately known as the Snout. But even Dr. Eiseley had to admit to "the eternal mystery, the careful finger of God," waving in the oozy pond of 300 million years ago. Still, no one told me "Why creation?" Why we are here—humanity, or humanity up from Eden, or humanity up from Snout.

So I moved on to the next question: If there is a God and if that God loves us and if that God is all-powerful, why would what happened to Alex Felini, what was happening to Riann Miles, happen? And not just them, but the millions and millions like them in circumstances of suffering, pain, disaster, evil? I mean, if God is all-powerful and all-loving, isn't that a fair question?

Sure; and just as unanswerable . . . just as unanswerable as my question of "Why creation?" But that didn't stop me from asking, either. Not any more. I had been hooked by the mystery, first through experience and now through mind. And I anticipate I'll never be unhooked until I see "face to face."

I was reading one snow-filled February evening, reading about God and pain and evil, when the telephone rang. I'm not big on being disturbed when I'm nestled. The telephone has rarely been my third ear. I debated answering it.

I did. Riann Miles was in the hospital. She had been admitted that morning. She didn't look good. Could I come and talk with her mother? She had been pretty upset earlier.

It was a three-north nurse.

"Sure, I'll be right there."

Not now. I'm not in the mood. Not now. Make it go away. I don't want to. Besides, I had talked with Riann's mother just a few days earlier and she told me then that the family, including Riann, was going to Jamaica at the end of February. She can't die before that. They need that one last trip. I don't feel like doing this. Not now. No.

It's a natural rebellion. The mind doesn't want to accept. What will I find? Will it make any difference anyway, my being there?

I walked part of the way to Children's, in the snow, all bundled up. I wanted to . . . to kick clumps of snow and crunch through untrod plots of white and be cold and wet . . . to fight with nature . . . to feel, outside.

But I got there just the same.

Riann was all right. Another false alarm; another labor pain in reverse. She was sitting up in bed eating cherry jello, wearing her red nightshirt with a big "STOP" sign on the front.

Appropriate.

"Hi, Nina!"

"Hi. How *are* you?"

"Fine. I didn't feel too good earlier, but I feel fine now. Dr. Jenssen says I can go home Tuesday maybe. That's not too bad, two days. Want some jello?"

"No thanks."

"Mommy brought Clive, but then she left him in the car! She

says he's sitting on the dashboard. He's gonna look awfully funny to people walking by," she giggled.

Mrs. Miles closed the door. "Want some wine?" Mrs. Miles was not all right. She opened the closet door and there was a half-gallon bottle of white wine. "Eric figured I'd need it. It beats jello."

Riann giggled.

We talked of pleasantries, the three of us, and drank wine, the two of us. Mrs. Miles was more tense than I had ever seen her. "Dr. Verdi gave me some Valium. He said I have to be more accepting, more placid. But really I can't any more." She stopped. It was hard to remember Riann's presence sometimes. Mrs. Miles did pretty well. "Old nervous Mommy," she laughed and got up and put her arms around the little girl in bed. "Good old Valium. They're better than my sleeping pills, Ri!"

"Yes!" Riann laughed. She began to tell the story again. How last summer after her first operation her mother was spending the night with her in the hospital. They were going to say prayers before bed. "But Mommy had taken a sleeping pill. They really work fast, I guess, because she kept falling asleep on the edge of my bed . . . in the middle of prayers! I would say, 'Mommy, it's your turn,' and she'd say, 'Let's pray silently tonight.' But I was sure she was falling asleep. And then she'd just keep saying how much she loves me, over and over again. I told her I love her, too; but she'd start all over again. I thought maybe she was sick or something. I almost called the nurse."

"But Mommy finally got to bed, didn't she, Ri? Dumb old Mommy," Mrs. Miles laughed again.

"Yes," laughed Riann, "she finally got to bed. But it really was a strange night." It was the third time, at least, that Riann had told me that story. I was to hear it several times again.

"Ri, is it OK if Nina and I get some coffee for a little? Will you rest? Then Mommy will come back and tuck you in."

"All right. See you later, Nina." We gave each other a big kiss.

Mrs. Miles told me how frightened she had been today. "I was sure this was it. Sure! She was *so* sick. She threw up the whole way here. I went through the whole thing in my mind, trying to accept, trying to resign myself that she was dying—now. I fell off the ledge . . . the whole way down. And I don't have the energy to pull myself up again. I just don't. Not knowing I'll have to go through it all over again. Someday. Soon . . . ?

"I'm glad she's alive, you know that," she went on, scrunching back on the three-north corridor window ledge; "you know what I mean. But to watch her be *so* sick, and know it still isn't the end. Will it be worse than this? Will she be in agony? Will she lie there like that little girl last winter—what was her name, in 378?"

"Pat Allen?"

"Pat Allen; that's it."

"I was hoping you hadn't seen her."

"I wish I hadn't. She was right across from Riann in December."

"Her tumor wasn't the same kind."

"I know. But I still see her lying there . . ."

So did I. But I didn't say that.

Mrs. Miles clenched her fingers. "I just want to ask 'Why, God? Why do this to her? Why do *this?* Why the agony?' It's not fair!" She paused. I waited.

"You know," she went on, "it's an awful thing to say, but I guess I'm just mad at God right now. Really angry. That's an awful thing to admit, and I'm sorry . . . But I can't help it. That's the way I feel."

That was it. On that window ledge that winter February Sunday, that was it. It all crashed together in my mind—Mrs. Felini: "Pray he'll die," bitterly; Alex: "But I hope you can understand . . . it still makes me mad"; Mrs. Miles: "Really angry." It was the missing link, the unacceptable acceptable, the negative feeling that no "moralizer" had the right, or the ability when all was said and done, to strip away: Anger—at God—in the face of unbearable, unexplainable suffering.

Guilt, bargaining, disbelief, depression—they are all normal feelings as long as they don't last an abnormal length of time and overcome the emotional balance of their subject. But anger— anger at God: It is there when everything else is stripped away, in the basement of the human gut.

It is an anger that asks, "Why am I human?" and "Why can't I stop what's happening?" and "Why don't I understand?" And it's an anger that says, "If I were God and I loved Riann the way everyone says You do, You can damn well bet I wouldn't let this happen to her!"

I wanted to shout, "Look! Revelation! I put some pieces to- gether! I understand something! I see a truth—for me; something that makes sense!" But the words that came out of my mouth sounded calm, as if I had said them a thousand times before.

But I hadn't.

"This may sound strange," I said, "but I'm glad you said that, about being angry at God. It's a normal, healthy reaction. It's focusing all your frustrations and mixed feelings where they really belong . . . saying, admitting, 'I'm helpless; I want to change things and I can't; but you can, God, so why don't you?!' There may be a part of you that never will be totally without anger at God. I don't know. But it's better than being angry at family or friends or doctors or other people. God can take it; he under- stands."

"Then I am normal? It isn't wrong, this feeling? I've felt it for a long time . . . but I didn't want to admit it. I mean, you're not supposed to get angry at God . . ."

"Jesus did." Where did that come from, I wondered? I hadn't been thinking it. Not at all.

Her eyes widened. Her mouth opened. She knew when. It had struck her, too. The Revelation. The truth that her feelings were justified. Her humanness, her personhood, was of value to God— her total personhood, including anger. Jesus Christ, in his death, among his dying words, had justified her in this moment.

For the first time in my life I *felt* Revelation. No, I can't explain it in words. And that, of course, gives validity to the reality of the "mystery." I had *read* about God in Jesus Christ participating in the human experience, participating in suffering, knowing rejection, knowing aloneness, knowing pain, knowing fear, knowing *anger*—anger at God? I had *read* it; but it had not been Revelation. Until now.

"Believe first, then you will understand." Dr. Davies had repeated it again and again. "Respond first, and then you will find . . . you will find that you already have been found."

I had believed. I had responded. I had read. But only now had I understood . . . just a fragment . . . a meteor—beautiful, bright, swift—blazing through the dark sky, then gone. But not gone.

A Revelation; a pinpoint of understanding never to be forgotten, nurtured and bundled in belief.

"I remember; you're right!" Mrs. Miles said. "It was just before he said, 'Father, into thy hands I commit my spirit.' Jesus did get angry! He did ask God why he had forsaken him. . . . And Jesus was our example, wasn't he . . . ?"

"Yes, he was." We didn't say any more, just sat on that window ledge. I'm not sure what she was thinking, but my mind was racing on . . . on . . . talking it out with myself. Yes, Christ was our example, a human being, participating in that which is human —pain, suffering, anger, and death . . . even death. Christ was God's own Son, and God didn't even save him from dying. Sure Jesus was angry—not with a vindictive anger, but with an anger that claimed the very intensity of his being; which is what I realized Mrs. Miles was doing now—claiming the very intensity of her being, her humanness. But she *wasn't* saying she felt *hopeless*. And Jesus wasn't either, when he asked, "My God, my God, why hast thou forsaken me?" He didn't say, "God, forget it; I don't need you." He didn't say, "God, I can go it alone." He didn't simply *stop talking,* as so many people do as they slip into the isolation of hopelessness. He cried out with a *"me"*. . . a "how could You do this to *me?"* Just as Mrs. Miles was doing, really.

But in the very object of the question, the very object of the anger—in God—came the *hope*, the knowledge of a love that "had been."

My mind wouldn't stop now. The fragment of Revelation was taking hold.

We don't get angry with someone for seeming to forsake us if we haven't been loved by that someone to begin with. And we don't get angry at all—and tell them so—if we don't have hope that that love still exists.

And the climax of this was on the cross. It is the mystery of grace, the mystery of faith, the mystery of God's unconditional love that will conquer all in the end that crept in in those moments on the cross between, "My God, my God, why hast thou forsaken *me?*" and "Father, into *thy* hands I commit my spirit."

It was Jesus' choice. God didn't dazzle him into it or manipulate him into it. And Jesus didn't say, "God, I'm sorry I got angry." It was *despite* his anger, *despite* his unanswered question, that Jesus chose not to go it alone.

Somehow, in those moments, Jesus realized the responsibility of his freedom. He realized in those moments that it wasn't up to God to choose him—God had already done that; but that it was now up to him to choose God, to claim in faith the love that stood beyond his anger, beyond his humanness, beyond his powerlessness, beyond his question that *remained unanswered:* "My God, my God, why hast thou forsaken me?"

Jesus Christ died on the cross, but his life, given to God, did not end. For in the final moments, in the darkest, deepest, cruelest, most painful moments—moments in which he had claimed, in anger, the very intensity of his being, and proved in fact that he was truly human—Jesus freely chose to return his spirit to God. And God, freely given back his power, snatched life from death eternally. The *"me"* became *"thy,"* and death became life in God.

And, I thought, today that same choice is up to you, Mrs. Miles, and to me, and to each of us. That's what our freedom as human beings is all about. I believe God loves each of us without condition, no matter what we ever do or say or think or feel, no matter what. His grace is not "cheap grace," but it's *free* grace, given freely in love. And we are free to accept that love, respond to that love—"Father, into thy hands I commit my spirit"—or reject that love and try to go it alone. It's up to us.

I breathed. Something had made sense. I had caught it. I wouldn't forget.

The look of revelation was still in Mrs. Miles's eyes. "My God, my God, why hast thou forsaken me?" and "Father, into thy hands I commit my spirit." That was all she had needed. And, after all, it is enough. That is it, those two feelings: "me" giving away to "thy." When we scrape away everything else—everything —that's what we as human beings, as Christian human beings, have left: anger and acceptance; anger and the free choice to respond . . . beyond our anger, beyond our unanswered questions, to God's everlasting, unconditional love. "Me" becomes "thy" and we are safe and free and upheld in more than our finite dreams can imagine.

It was quiet in the hallway. The lights were dim and the courtyard beneath the window was dark and full of snow. Only the whir of a floor polisher in a distant corridor could be heard.

Reading words is vital. But alone, it's not enough. Meditation on written words is good. But alone, it's not enough. At least for me it was not enough.

Do when you don't want to do.

Go when you don't want to go.

Plod through the snow.

Kick fresh clumps of frozen white.

Wrestle with cold and wind.

Go when you don't want to go . . . and when you least expect it, you may glimpse through the open door to Revelation. That was my lesson that cold February night several years ago . . . a winter night above other winter nights.

Sometimes, when you experience a certain feeling, do you believe that everyone around you is feeling the same thing? I had wondered that about Riann's mother late that same Sunday night. Just because I had put pieces together in my mind that evening did I just imagine that she had too?

"I had to thank you for last night." The phone had rung early Monday morning. "All of what you said meant a lot. But the part about Jesus being angry, and then putting himself into God's hands anyway . . . That's what I remember most. I talked with my sister in California last night after you left and told her. It meant a lot to her, too."

Yes, I was embarrassed in a strange way. But yes, I was glad Mrs. Miles had called. It was something I needed to know, an affirmation of a feeling, an affirmation of a direction, an affirmation of meaning and interpretation. An affirmation.

Maybe Jesus was reciting the twenty-second Psalm. "My God, my God, why . . . ?" But wasn't the psalmist angry, too? And why *that* Psalm? Why else if it was not indicative of his mood?

24.

There's an anecdote I forgot to tell earlier about Manuelito Cerci's mother.

One day after Manuelito's surgery we were sitting in the waiting room talking. Mrs. Cerci interjected suddenly, with a very puzzled look on her face, "What is an ascidulator?"

"A what?"

"An ascidulator?"

"I've never heard of it; I don't know," I shook my head

and shrugged my shoulders. "Can you spell it?"

"No . . ."

"Can you use it in a sentence? Sentence . . . ?"

"Ah, si. Doctor, come in Manuelito's room. Smile. Examine Manuelito. Smile. Ask one, two question. Smile. Say 'ascidulator.' "

I paused for a moment to let the sentence sink in . . . then burst out laughing. So did two other mothers sitting there. Mrs. Cerci looked puzzled. "I'm sorry," I apologized, still gasping for air. "It's an American saying. Four [I held up four fingers], four words. 'I'll—I will—[she nods] see you later.' " In other words, the doctor will return again sometime soon."

"Oh! I see," said Mrs. Cerci, relieved. " 'I'll see you later!' " She laughed now too.

Sometimes it's a good thing our minds protect us enough that we can't think about what we're doing as we're doing it. Afterwards, yes; but not during.

It was that way for me the two weeks Riann died. If I had stopped to think about *what* was happening, about what I was doing . . . stopped to think about it for very long . . . I wonder if I could have done it. Even now, nearly a month later, my mind will let me *feel* only a little bit. I can recite what happened. But I still can't feel the total impact.

I'm glad for that.

It was Thursday, the Thursday before Easter. I had seen Riann, had spent the day with her, just one day earlier. Now she was in the hospital, dying. She would not go home again.

I had a sandwich, a Coke, and a television set—it was one of those evenings. My telephone rang at seven P.M. It was a nurse from three-north. Riann had been admitted.

She went on to describe her condition. But I stopped hearing with the word "admitted." It was as if I couldn't find a place in my brain to absorb the additional information. It just kept tumbling around with no home.

I finally asked the nurse to stop talking a minute.

"I just saw her yesterday, spent the day with her." I repeated it.

"Yes?" she said. "Well, she's here now and she doesn't look good at all. I just thought you'd want to know."

"Thank you."

I hung up. I went back to my sandwich, my Coke, and my television. The information was still tumbling about. No home.

The phone rang again, ten minutes later. I hadn't moved. It was another nurse from three-north, the same information.

"I just thought you'd want to know. I told Mrs. Miles I would call you."

"Thank you."

Back to the TV, the Coke, and the sandwich.

I decided not to go to the hospital that evening. The second nurse, Jennifer Bradford, had said she didn't think Riann would die that night. And with both her parents there, I didn't want to be the "minister of death," hovering. That was my rationalization. But I don't know if it was my reason. Maybe I just couldn't absorb it. Maybe I just couldn't accept it. The *now*ness.

The other shoe had dropped.

It was just one day earlier, Wednesday, that we had had such a good time, Riann and her mother and I.

But I saw then that she had weakened, considerably, since I had seen her before their trip to Jamaica. Her right eye teared a lot and her right side drooped and she was terribly, terribly thin, wasted.

But nonetheless, she was happy—unbelievably happy. From the time I walked in that Wednesday she didn't stop talking. She had on a little blue and white jersey dress and a bow in her hair and heavy brown Buster Brown shoes and white socks. She was sitting propped up in the corner of the red and green sofa in the playroom. She had thrown up her lunch just before I arrived and she was afraid I would notice the smell on her breath when I kissed her.

"Nope, I can't smell a thing. [I couldn't.] And besides, you don't think a thing like that would keep me from kissing you, do you?!"

She giggled.

She had her program all set, things she wanted to say and do. First, she wanted to give me the gift she had brought from Jamaica.

"Do you like to munch on things . . . like when you're concentrating on your work and you're not really thinking?" she asked.

"No, not usually?"

"Well, I just wanted to warn you not to munch on these!" She handed me some seed and nut beads wrapped in tissue paper. " 'Cause they're poison!" She giggled.

"Oh! I'll remember! Riann, they're really pretty!" I put them on and gave her a big kiss.

Her mother had fixed us a drink and was sitting on the chair next to me at the other end of the sofa.

"Thank you again for the beanbag chair," Riann continued with the next thing on her agenda. "We tried to get me in it, but I guess I'll have to wait until I can bend a little better! But I really love it a lot. I can hardly wait to tell Dr. Verdi that I have *my own* beanbag chair and I don't have to sit in his any more!"

Giggle. Giggle.

Talk about the ironies of life . . . I had ordered the red beanbag chair for Riann for Valentine's Day. Not that her parents couldn't afford it. Not that she'd get a lot of use out of it. But simply because it was *doing* something to make her happy, to add a little bit.

Twice at least she had mentioned how much she wanted a

beanbag chair "like Dr. Verdi's." She had said it to me in conversation; not as a hint—she wasn't like that—just as a stream
of consciousness. I happened by one in a department store in
late January and decided to order it for Riann for Valentine's
Day. *Then* she still could have sat in it, enjoyed it a little bit
more . . .

But it didn't come. And it didn't come. The saleslady had
casually promised delivery in "five days." That would have been
February 4. This was April, nearly mid-April. When weeks
dragged on I asked the saleslady to telephone me when it came
in. I didn't want it delivered "after the fact." On April 5 someone
called. "Your red beanbag chair is in! Shall we deliver it? By the
way, the card reads, 'Happy Valentine's Day.' Should we change
it to 'Happy Easter'?"

"Sure, 'Happy Easter!' "

I almost didn't have it sent. I sensed it wasn't very long. But
what the heck. It wasn't Riann's fault she was dying.

The tickled look on her face that Wednesday was enough. She
had enjoyed it. It was all hers, her very own.

But I wanted to wring someone's neck at that department
store.

You can't buy it, can you? . . . Time . . .

"How was your trip?"

"That's next! I want to tell you about that, and
then show you the pictures, and then read you a funny book, and
then we'll have lunch, and then we'll go to school . . . if you want
to, that is?"

"Sure."

"Good!"

She did . . . everything. She told me about her trip and showed
me the beautiful pictures and told me how Kevin and Eric "drank
so much beer they got sick . . . especially Eric—he threw up! And
Mommy said she could hear him and Kevin in the bathroom
. . . and then trying to clean things up . . . and she laughed."

And she told about the calypso singer who sang about someone with a brain tumor in his head and how the doctor had to take it out and how she laughed and pointed to her head when he sang it and how everybody probably thought she and her family were "crazy!"

And she told me about her aunt Meg who came with them on the trip and how funny she was. And about the live animals on the lawn outside her Jamaica hotel room. And she showed me a "funny" picture of her waking up in the morning "still half asleep."

Then she read me *The Elephant and Grape Book*—all of it! Giggling and laughing and having fun, nonstop. I forgot she was sick. I forgot she was dying. We just had fun.

We had lunch, then put her wheelchair in the back of the station wagon and drove off to school. It was a small private day school that looked like a rambling old army barracks with atmosphere. Four little boys, about nine years old, ran out and gallantly helped lift Riann in her wheelchair up the few steps into the school.

We went into a "communications" room where the children were using various communication aids. Riann introduced me to her classmates as the "writer of the Clive stories." (She had taken one to school for the class to read.) She was still happy and cheerful.

Then we went into a room to watch a special television program on ballet. Riann was wheeled to the front and her mother and I sat in the back.

The television was terribly loud. It kept pounding and pounding in my ears. How could Riann stand it, I wondered, being so close?

But Riann was being bothered by something more than the television. Her tumor had changed, or moved, or done something . . . at least that's what must have happened . . .

A little boy came up to us. "Mrs. Miles, Riann wants you. She's upset."

The little girl was in tears. She wanted to go home. Her head hurt.

I was glad to get out of the loud room, but not when I saw Riann. It was unlike her. She was sobbing and sobbing and making sounds of pain. I got sick in my stomach.

We tried to get her parka on her. "My head hurts. Oh, my head hurts. It hurts." She sobbed and sobbed.

Finally we got her into the car. But the pain didn't stop. "It was probably the confusion," said her mother. "Too many people. She seems to get upset when she's around too many people all at once. Too much confusion. But I don't think I've seen it quite this bad," she added to me as she slipped into the front seat beside Riann.

I had never seen Riann upset by confusion, so I had to take her mother's word for it. But her cries certainly scared me. To me, she looked like she was in pain, in agony. I guess my face showed my fright to Mrs. Miles.

Riann sobbed all the way home. We tried to calm her, but we couldn't. I did notice some change in the sound, though. More from pain to a need to get settled, to get quiet. Maybe it had been that way all along, the confusion.

Whatever, she did stop crying, did calm down, when we got her home. Her mother carried her in to "Daddy's side of the bed" where she could "rest" a little. In a few minutes she seemed fairly comfortable.

"Could I please have my schoolbooks? My math?" she asked.

"Sure, darling." Her mother gave her her books. "Now you just rest. Mommy has to get the car pool. It'll only take a few minutes. But Nina will be here with you if you want anything."

She turned to me as we left the bedroom. "I know it sounds awful, but I have the car pool today and the kids are waiting right now. There's no way to get anyone else. I'm sure she'll be all right. She's calm now. I'll be back in ten minutes. Do you mind?"

"No! Go ahead; I understand. We'll be fine."

My knees went weak. I went back into the bedroom.

"How do you feel?"

"OK, thank you. My head feels much better."

"Can I get you something?"

"No, thank you. I'm just working on my math. I have more trouble with math. I don't know why. Are these right?" She showed me some addition. Thank goodness it wasn't "new math"!

"Yes, all but this one. Three and three and three equals eight, doesn't it?"

She hesitated a minute, then broke into a wide grin. "You're funny! It's nine!"

"Oh, I'll be! Well, I never was good at math, either."

She giggled.

"I'll let you rest. If you want anything, I'll be in the den, just call." (The den was next to the master bedroom, where Riann was.)

I just made it to the sofa before my knees gave out. I sat for a few minutes, then found the liquor cabinet. There are times when liquor *is* medicine, and this was one of them. I drank a glass of white wine and sat with clenched muscles, listening.

But all went well. Mrs. Miles was back in ten minutes. She found Riann comfortable and resting. "No more headaches."

Neither of us could talk for a bit. She was as shaken—or more so—than I.

A few minutes later Riann wanted to get up. So her mother wheeled her to the den for a bit, then into the playroom to join her little sister, who had returned from school a few minutes earlier. (I can still see Riann sitting in that wheelchair by the den door, in her little blue dress with the matching bow in her hair. But her face was not the same. She was holding back pain. I'm not saying that because I know what happened the next day. I knew it then. The pain showed through.)

Finally Mrs. Miles and I had about ten minutes to relax, to unwind a bit. But we still were in shock, I think.

When Mr. Miles came home I realized for the first time how

late it was. The three of us talked for a few minutes, then Riann was wheeled out to the front door to say good-bye. The look of pain was still there.

I thanked her for a nice day, said I hoped she felt better, and wished her a happy Easter.

But tears formed in her eyes. "She doesn't want you to go," said her mother. "Good-byes are getting harder and harder for her.

"Wish Nina a happy Easter, dear."

She did. But it didn't come out well. She kissed me and her eyes were heavy with tears. Then she looked away.

I felt empty, strange. I hadn't expected it. Maybe she knew about tomorrow. Maybe she knew the whole thing, and we were fooling ourselves. Maybe she really did know she was dying. Maybe she was just too kind to tell us, to drag us through it . . .

Or maybe it was just the pain. Or maybe just not wanting to see a good day end.

We'll never know.

I got up at eight A.M. on Good Friday. I could have been at Children's, in Riann's room, by nine-thirty. But I moved like wet cement, holding back. An unrealness had set in. I was operating by radar.

Finally dressed and ready, I decided to stop by my church on the way—not to attend the noon Good Friday services—but just to sit, quietly.

But in my church there was nowhere to sit quietly, not after about five minutes. The ushers started arriving in the old gothic sanctuary and their echoes of greeting rolled down the empty rows and bounced off the concrete walls. They bustled about, being efficient.

Of course it was normal.

But my world wasn't normal any longer. It had changed . . . like never quite before. Someone I loved was dying.

I couldn't stand the "normal" noise. I went to a small chapel, one recently redecorated in polychrome and beauty. Here it would be quiet. I could think.

But someone was practicing the organ. It wasn't fair! It was my church! Why couldn't I find quiet in my own church?

There is no such thing, of course, as "my own church."

Riann was in room 381, the room she had been in when she had her second operation, the morning she waved "Bye, Nina," the morning the "play lady" and I had come early, the morning just over one year ago.

I knocked on the closed door. "Come in." It was a whisper, as the knock had been.

Inside it was dark, the shade pulled, the lights off. Riann's mother was there with two neighbors. All was hushed.

"Hi, come in. Riann just fell asleep. She had a bad night. Here, give me your coat. You remember Mary Alice Krider and Betty Armstrong?"

"Yes, hi," I whispered. Then I had a chance to look at Riann. I went numb. She was lying on her left side. Her spine and her neck were arched back so drastically that she formed a "C." Her knees were bent up. "She can't straighten them," her mother said. "She can't straighten anything. She can't get her head any farther forward than that. Dr. Verdi says it's the pressure from the tumor."

"Oh."

Riann was wearing a pink and blue checked flannel nightgown

with a ruffled bodice and ruffled sleeves. She looked so frail, like a sleeping flower. The change in two days was overwhelming.

There was no doubt she was dying.

The only questions now were "How long?" and "How much worse?" and "How much pain?" and "How much agony?" The same old questions. Only now the answers were coming. The "when?" had become "now."

It was 12:45 P.M. Mrs. Miles asked me if I had had lunch. "Yes." (I hadn't, but I didn't want any.)

"Mary Alice has to go soon. She and I were going to go down and get some lunch and Betty was going to stay with Riann, but now that you're here, would you mind? That way Betty can come now and then she can get home too. She's been here—they both have, bless their hearts—all morning. Can you stay for a while? Or do you have somewhere to go, too?"

"No, I'm fine. I have no plans. I'll stay with Riann now. You go on to lunch."

"You're sure you don't mind?"

"No, not at all."

"I don't think she'll wake up. She needs some sleep. She was awake with me most of the night."

"OK."

"If anything happens, we'll be in the coffee shop. Dr. Verdi thinks it will be soon, but not likely for a day or two . . ."

They left to get lunch. I sat on the chair by the bed and looked at Riann. I wasn't feeling anything.

As I had opened the door I had wondered if it would be the same, our closeness—or what I felt was our closeness—now that the chips were down. Or would the family draw inward? It was possible. I was prepared to sense it, to leave gracefully, to not intrude.

But it wasn't that way. When I walked into that dark room that Good Friday afternoon, I became part of the process. And from that point on, I was unable to think about *what* was happening. I was just there. The mind is a fantastic protector at times . . . a friend.

I looked at Riann and didn't feel anything. Maybe it was shock. But I was numb. I just sat on the wooden chair looking at her face through the metal bed railing.

She opened her eyes. "Hi, Nina." She smiled.

"Hi, Riann. How do you feel?"

"OK, I guess. Where's Mommy?"

"Your mommy and Mrs. Krider and Mrs. Armstrong went to get a bite of lunch. Do you want me to call her? She should be back in a few minutes."

"No, that's OK. When did you come?"

"Oh, about a half hour ago. You were asleep. At least you weren't snoring!"

Giggle. "I bet you didn't expect to see me again so soon!"

"No, I sure didn't! I like to see you, mind you; but couldn't we pick a better spot than here?"

Giggle. "Yeah, you're right! Could I please have some water? Mommy had some in a cup with a syringe."

"Oh, I see it. It looks warm. Do you want me to get some fresh, with some ice?"

"That would be nice. Thank you."

I got some ice water in the ice room at the end of the hall.

"I had trouble with the straw last night, so Jennifer suggested Mommy use the syringe. It works much better, doesn't it?"

"Yes, that was a good idea."

(The "syringe" was just that, just like ones attached to shot needles, only without the needle and bigger than the average syringe. Instead of the needle, there was a small hole at the end. Liquids could be drawn into the syringe and then pushed back out through the hole and into the patient's mouth by depressing the sliding center stopper—just like a shot. It did work well. But what a weird thing to be doing . . . dropping water into Riann's mouth through a syringe. One more human dignity out the window. But she didn't seem to mind. She just accepted it as fact. No complaints. If she could accept it, I guess I could.)

"That's enough, thank you. That was good. Did you know that Jennifer went to Jamaica this morning?"

"Yes. She's really lucky!"

"I hope she has as nice a time as we did there."

"I do too. I'm glad you had such a nice time."

"So am I. I want to go back someday. It was so pretty. What time is it, please?"

"Just about 1:30."

"Clive is here. Do you see him?"

"Yes. Who's his friend?" A stuffed doll in a pink plaid dress sat smiling beside Clive on the window ledge.

"Oh, that's Mrs. McPatches. I've had her for a while, too. A friend of mine has one just like her, only hers has brown hair."

"She's cute."

"Thank you."

I was amazed at her conversation. Granted, it was weaker and slower than I had heard before, but it was still Riann. The tumor hadn't gotten to her mind, to her disposition.

"I didn't sleep too well last night. My neck sort of hurt. Maybe I'll try to go back to sleep now."

"OK, that's a good idea. I'll be here if you want anything. And Mommy will be back soon."

She fell asleep. I sat on the wooden desk chair that Mrs. Miles had placed by the side of her bed.

All the private rooms at University Children's were much the same, reasonable in size and reasonably well furnished. As you walked into Riann's room, there was a bed to your left, its head-board in the middle of the left wall. Next to it on the same wall was a daybed which lined the wall lengthwise and flush. In the daytime it served as a sort of sofa, with a wooden built-in backrest that opened to reveal a pillow. Opposite the door was a window. An orange vinyl chair with matching stool sat underneath. A radiator was behind the chair. Directly to the right of the doorway was a closet, then a natural wood desk and matching chair, and finally the bathroom door, all three along the same right wall. The bathroom was white tile and contained a sink and toilet.

The walls were yellow. A six-inch strip of flowered paper ran

around the top edges of the walls, next to the ceiling. The spread
on the daybed was green. Riann's junior bed was shiny chrome.
Its top and bottom adjusted up and down by turning knobs
underneath. Above the bed against the wall were several lights
and a nurse-call-button. Behind the orange vinyl chair was a floor
lamp. And over the desk was a framed picture of children at a
carnival.

I knew Riann would die here, in room 381. When? Today—
Good Friday? Tomorrow? Easter Sunday? Somehow it seemed
the ordeal wouldn't last beyond Easter. Symbolic. I guess I wasn't
the only one thinking that.

"Wouldn't you know it would be Holy Thursday, Good Friday,
Easter," said Mrs. Miles about an hour later when we were sitting
in the room talking. Riann was still asleep.

"I thought about that," I said.

"I've thought about it a lot. It really brings home what you and
I were talking about last February. It's almost like God planned
it this way.

"She's much better now than she was last night, though," Mrs.
Miles continued. "She really looked awful, and had a lot of pain
in her neck. But they aren't going to let her have pain any more;
not if they can help it. Dr. Verdi promised me that.

"But they aren't going to do anything extra, either. Just let the
inevitable happen as quickly as possible. I can't stand to see her
like this. I don't want to keep her any longer if this is the price
she has to pay."

The acceptance was there. For the duration, there were no
more questions. Not for either of us. We had worked it through.
I knew I had. And now I knew she had, too.

Grief and emptiness and the real realization of the magnitude
of what had happened—to Riann, to us—would come. It wasn't
all cut and dried. But from now until she died we each knew we'd
make it.

. . . If it just didn't take too long.

. . . Or bring uncontrollable pain.

. . . If . . .

Mrs. Miles was exhausted. Dr. Verdi had told her to go home, to spend Friday night at home. He said he didn't think Riann would die that night.

She wanted to. But still she was afraid to leave, afraid to leave Riann alone.

This time it was different. This time we were close enough, had shared enough—Mrs. Miles and Riann and I—that I could offer.

"I'd like to stay."

"Oh, we couldn't ask you to do that. If she's like last night, you won't get any sleep at all."

"I'm prepared for that. Please. I want to."

"Well, Dr. Verdi doesn't want me to stay. He said if I start staying at night, soon—if there is a soon—I won't be any good at all, for Riann or the other children or Eric or me . . . or anybody. I hate to leave her . . . But I suppose he's right.

"But do you *really* want to? I'm sure the nurses will look in on her often. That's asking a lot, for you to stay. I know you won't get much sleep."

"Don't worry about me. I had today off from work so I was able to sleep later this morning, and I can go home tomorrow afternoon and go to sleep."

"OK, if you're sure. I would feel a lot better . . ."

"I'm sure."

I took a bus home, picked up a nightgown and toothbrush and a pair of slippers and returned to Children's. Mrs. Miles was going to leave with Mr. Miles soon after he arrived at the hospital from his office. If they had gone by the time I returned, she said, they would leave a note if there was any new information.

It was warmish out and sort of humid that April Good Friday evening. The world looks different when your eyes are not only yours, but surrogate for someone who is dying. I looked at the Lake. It was glassy blue dissolving into a pink sky. Boats weren't out yet, and the Lake lay undisturbed in the setting sun's reflection. Riann would never see it again: not see the boats this summer, not make her second trip to Jamaica, not see another squirrel, or bird . . . or grow up to love a man . . .

Well, most of the time I didn't think about *what* was happening . . .

The Mileses had gone when I returned to Children's. I opened the door to room 381. The bright light over Riann's bed was on. But I didn't see Riann.

A knife slashed through my stomach. Tiny needles pricked my whole body.

Finally I moved closer. She was there, sleeping! But the bed had been turned around so her head was now where her feet had been that afternoon. She was all covered up, a blanket was over the head railing, and since her knees were bent, all I had been able to see from the door was the empty bottom of the bed!

I sat down . . . on the edge of the orange vinyl stool . . . a long time.

Riann was asleep. The overhead fluorescent lamp was very bright. But perhaps she had wanted it on? I left it.

I put my night things and trench coat in the closet and sat on the orange vinyl chair. I realized it squeaked each time it was sat upon, and I was afraid the noise would awaken Riann. But it didn't.

I sat for a long time without thinking, barely breathing. Just looking at Riann in her little pink and blue checked flannel nightgown.

She slept peacefully. So much so that I began to listen for her breathing. I couldn't hear it! What if she had died in those few moments I had been sitting on the orange vinyl chair? What if she had just stopped breathing?

I was frightened. I got up to look. Her chest was moving, up and down.

I carefully sat back down.

What if she had died? What then? It wasn't that I wasn't prepared. I think I was, as much as possible. But I didn't want her to. Not while I was there, alone. Selfish? Perhaps. But I still didn't want her to. Not while I'm with you alone, Riann. Please don't die while I'm with you alone . . .

"With you alone." Taken apart from the rest of the sentence, that didn't make sense. And then it just didn't make sense at all. For we were not alone, either of us. My panic lessened.

I looked at the little milk-white face, the little neck bent back so far, the thick black lashes, the pink lips, the soft brown hair . . . a fuzzy blanket over a brain tumor that was winning. I looked at the sleeping child . . . and realized how close, how very close she was to the answer, to knowing for sure about God, about transcendence, about life . . . knowing the secret . . .

> But when winter comes, my little one will *know its secret*
>   —Of life, of love of rebirth,
> And winter will be *her* gift glorious.
>   For she will see Your face; while I still wait and dream
>   And cry on naked branches.

As I realized this in that quiet, blue-bright room, I sensed that the agony, somehow, was worth it. No, it wasn't *my* agony, *my* brain rumor, *my* suffering . . . *my* death.

But for a fleeting moment, part of me wished it was . . . wished for the secret.

My mind reached randomly beyond my experience . . . "Just think," I wanted to say to Riann, "soon you'll *see* God, soon you'll know more than your mommy and your daddy and your brothers and sister and I can wildly imagine . . . soon . . ."

The reality of pain was put aside for a sense of awe in those moments in that room. Part of the awe was fear—fear that Riann really would die soon, like that evening, that night. Part of the awe was the mystery—the mystery of death, and life, and hereafter, and God. Part of the awe was faith—faith in a love that is unconditional despite our unanswered questions, a love that keeps its promise, a love that will *never* let us go . . . a love this is God.

And in the face of that awe, in those first moments with Riann that Friday night, the anger was gone. It was pushed aside, pushed out. I *knew* there was a God who was good, and a heaven—a hereafter where "there shall be no more death, neither sorrow, nor crying, neither shall there by any more pain: for the former things are passed away." (Rev. 21:4, KJV) "And they shall see his face; and his name shall be in their foreheads. And there shall be no night there; and they need no candle, neither light of the sun; for the Lord God giveth them light: and they shall reign for ever and ever." (Rev. 22:4–5, KJV)

But then, when someone you love is dying . . . heaven is a reality . . .

No! It was more than that, more powerful than a not wanting to let go into nothingness. For me, through Riann, it was the assurance, confirmed again.

Other times and other places, the anger would return in my humanness. But hopefully, ultimately, I will not forget the assurance . . .

> For I am persuaded, that neither death, nor life, nor angels, nor principalities, nor powers, nor things present, nor things to come, Nor height, nor depth, nor any other creature, shall be able to separate us from the love of God, which is in Christ Jesus our Lord.
>
> [Rom. 8:38–39, KJV]

I don't know how long I sat in that orange vinyl chair. I don't know to what reaches my mind roamed. I do know you must respect those moments if you respect me. For I was journeying on untried soil. And as I write this I discover that the mystery is aided in its preservation by the inadequacy of words. Fortunately, we can grasp more than words can describe.

More than one year now has passed since Riann died. Most of the preceding pages were written long ago. And they have remained unchanged, as testimony to edges of feeling and to the embryo chaplain, and as a reminder of the worth of discovery.

But despite the passage of time, I find that these last pages are to be written from a memory still almost too personal to commit to type. I have put off these pages until time has run out. They must be written. But I shall deny the task while doing it.

I had thought that with time writing about Riann's death would become less personal. But it hasn't. I do not yet want to share it with you. But I must trust you enough to trust that you will understand. Though, forgive me, I cannot yet believe you will . . .

Riann awoke. She said her mommy had told her I was going to spend the night and she was glad. Though she certainly hoped, for both our sakes, that she would be able to get more sleep tonight than she had last!

She decided she wanted the bright lights off. I was glad. And maybe she could eat some cherry jello. And then she would try to get some more sleep.

As I was feeding the jello to her she asked me why her leg hurt so. "It never did before; not like this . . ."

"I don't know for sure, Riann. Why don't you ask Dr. Verdi tomorrow? But I do know that while you've been sleeping you've kicked your knees against the metal bed railing a number of times. Maybe you just bruised yourself?"

"Maybe that's it . . ."

"Why don't I get some blankets and cover the railing where your knees are. Then maybe it won't hurt so much."

"That's a good idea . . . Kevin has a friend who has muscular dystrophy. He's in a wheelchair all the time . . . But he doesn't seem to mind. He's always happy . . ."

"That's good."

Later that night I wondered at her train of thought. Was she afraid *she* had muscular dystrophy? Was that why she went from her leg hurting to Kevin's friend? It hadn't struck me at all at the moment. Maybe I didn't want it to . . .

What if she did ask, I thought. *The Question:* "Nina, am I dying?" or "Nina, am I going to die?" God, help me. I tried to think of an answer. But I couldn't. I couldn't anticipate the setting, the circumstances. I would just have to grit my teeth and pray for the "right" words . . . if it happened.

Riann fell asleep. Slowly, I felt more free to move about quietly. I checked her breathing a bit less often. I wasn't quite as afraid the "baby would break if I picked it up," so to speak.

I telephoned Mr. and Mrs. Miles to tell them all was well— it's amazing what "relatively speaking" can come to mean—and went back to Riann's room. She was still asleep.

I changed into my night clothing and pulled down the covers on the daybed and got out the pillow. Only the night light was on in the room. A street lamp outside was pouring orange light through the window.

My interlude of mental floating was over. I was back to not feeling, not thinking, just doing. I was beginning—though I didn't know it then—what was to become a routine.

Riann awakened as I was brushing my hair.

"Nina?"

"Yes, sweetheart?"

"Do you think there's any more cherry jello?"

"I don't know, but I'll check. Do you want anything else?"

"No, just that, thank you."

"OK, I'll be right back."

I put on my robe. The jello was there. I returned and began to feed her.

She was feeling better. It was obvious. "You know, when I was little one time Eric and Kevin and Allison and I went out and we were with my cousin and he ordered a hamburger and 'wrench-wries.' " She giggled. "He was too little to say 'french fries,' so he said 'wrench-wries.' So after that, when we were alone with just us, we always teased and said 'wrench-wries,' too. But we didn't tease him." She giggled again, remembering.

We talked and she ate her cherry jello and the street lamp watched.

"Nina, do you think I can get up tomorrow?"

I almost dropped the jello. "I hope so, Ri. We'll see how you feel. OK?"

"OK. I sure hope I can . . ."

"Me too."

A nurse came to turn Riann and straighten the sheets and wish her good-night. I slipped into the daybed.

She woke up several times afterwards, but all in all, she didn't seem to have too bad a night. When she did awaken it was from pain, in her neck. Usually, she would ask me to move her head or move her pillow or sometimes turn her. I felt OK about doing the first two, but I would call a nurse if she needed to be turned.

I slept, but lightly. I realized for the first time how a mother actually can sleep, yet hear her restless child in the next room. It's strange.

Riann would always say "thank you" and "please." Despite the pain, she would think to say "thank you" and "please"—to the nurses, to the doctors, to her family, to me, to everyone. She never forgot. Not once.

Saturday morning came "later" for Riann. The last time she had awakened had been about 5:30 A.M. and now it was 8:30 A.M. and she was still asleep. Thank goodness! I got up about 7:30, sink-bathed, dressed, and went to the nursing station for some coffee.

I telephoned Riann's mother about eight o'clock and told her how the night had gone. She said she would come in about eleven and I said I would stay until then. We both agreed I didn't have to. But we both knew I would.

About an hour later, Riann took a turn for the worse. I was giving her some cherry jello for breakfast and she was in mid-sentence, saying that eating all this jello was like being on a diet.

"But I love . . ." Her eyes slipped back in her head and her tongue shot out and back and her lips shook and her head and her right side jerked: a seizure. It scared the life out of me. I ran into the hall and called Mary Cooke, who was walking in my direction. She turned stark white and ran. She took one look at Riann. "She's seizing." She looked at her watch, and rubbed Riann's arm, and said, "It's all right, Riann, don't be frightened. It's OK."

She turned to me. "Scared you, huh?" I nodded. "They are scary. When did she start?"

"Just now."

"I think she's lost consciousness."

Riann kept on seizing. Five minutes. She seized nonstop for five minutes. Then she was fine.

"What happened?" Riann opened her eyes and asked a bit groggily.

"You had a little seizure," Mary explained. "But everything's OK. How do you feel?"

"A little funny, but OK. My tongue feels funny."

"That's from the seizure." Mary turned to me, quietly, aside, "I don't think in her position there's any danger of her swallowing her tongue. But I'll get you a wrapped depressor. If she does it again—and I have a feeling she will—just hold her tongue with it. It may help keep it from getting too sore. I'll get her medication in a syringe. You can give it to her with her breakfast."

It was scary. I hoped Riann wouldn't seize any more. She did. Five minutes later. For four minutes. But this time she didn't lose consciousness. And the tongue depressor annoyed her and scared her. "It's OK," said Mary. "I have a feeling her tongue will get sore regardless. She's not going to stop this."

(And she didn't. Soon, even it became routine. Sometimes Riann would even try to talk while seizing, try to finish a sentence. Her tongue did hurt, though. I would hold a cold wet rag on her lips while she seized. It seemed to help. Then we'd just pick up talking where we had left off. What else could we do?)

I didn't go home at all Saturday, to freshen up or anything. I don't remember details of the day, but I do remember that our tension mounted with the number of Riann's seizures. They had been a shock for Mrs. Miles, and a worse shock for Mr. Miles, who came in mid-afternoon. I left them alone with Riann.

About 5:30 P.M., as I was sitting reading in the small room behind the nursing station, Mrs. Miles came to the glass partition and motioned to me. "Eric is going across the street to bring back some martinis. Do you want one—or two?"

"Sure."

"Come sit with us while he's gone. You didn't have to leave, you know."

"I know. Thank you."

Ten minutes later, Mr. Miles returned with a dejected look on his face. "It's against the law. You can't take out drinks! I never knew that."

"Neither did I," Mrs. Miles and I said both at once.

They had brought Riann's dinner but she hadn't eaten much. Now she was asleep, had been for an hour or so, in between seizures.

"You know, let's all go out to dinner. Let's just go. We have to get away a bit." Mr. Miles was right.

"I'll ask Riann's nurse to keep a special eye on her," said Mrs. Miles. "She does seem to be sleeping well. And if she wakes up, the nurse can tell her Nina is coming back soon. Anyway, her nurse this evening is Cheri, and Riann really likes her. We *do* have to get out. All of us!"

I couldn't disagree. It was hard to go from quiet panic to unwinding to quiet panic to unwinding. Sooner or later you had to jump off the treadmill for a few minutes.

We went to a French restaurant and had our martinis—plural. Definitely plural. And we talked. We went through a sort of eulogy and mourning and laundering of our nerves. We were on an island in the middle of land, unaware of our surroundings, yet using tools of those surroundings to help keep us in perspective.

Life was still going on. At the backs of our minds somewhere, we remembered that.

When I returned to Children's, Riann still was asleep. Cheri said she had awakened several times, but seemed to be feeling better. Only three seizures. She had had some Coke and some cherry jello, too.

I got a book, crunched into the orange vinyl chair, and read.

"Nina, are you there?"

"Yes, Riann, I'm back. What is it sweetheart?" I got up.

"May I please get up?"

"Do you really feel like it, Ri?"

"Yes, please, in the wheelchair."

"OK, let me ask Cheri. We'll see what she says."

"You're kidding! She really wants to get up? I don't believe it!"

"Ask her yourself. I didn't believe it either."

It was a slow, painful process, but Riann finally was sitting up in her wheelchair—on top of two pillows and in front of two folded blankets for support. Her head tilted back far.

Cheri put a pillow behind her neck for support. Riann's body would no longer bend to fit a chair.

But she was up! And it made her *so* happy . . . for about three minutes. Then the pain came—real, horrid pain, by the look of her face.

Cheri was just finishing changing the sheets on her bed.

"Nina, may I please get back in bed now?"

"Sure, Riann, right away. Does it hurt?"

"Yes . . ."

I could see how much in her eyes. Dammit! She was so happy, so proud that I could "tell Mommy and Daddy when you call that I was up in my chair!"

But what did I expect? *She was dying.* It wasn't false labor pains any more. But Riann just wouldn't give up her personhood without a fight—so much so that those around her could actually begin to forget the truth, could almost come to accept things like seizures as "routine." Good for her!

Do not go gentle into that good night,

. . . .

Rage, rage against the dying of the light.
                              [Dylan Thomas]

We got her back into bed. But it took a long time to get her comfortable. Finally, she was.

"Shall I call Mommy and Daddy now?"

"Yes, please. Tell them I was up . . ."

"I won't forget. That will be the first thing on the list. Do you want anything before I go?"

"No, thank you. I'll try to sleep."

"OK. Ri, that was fantastic, getting up that way. You really are brave." I kissed her.

"Thank you. I wanted to stay longer. But it kind of hurt. Maybe tomorrow . . ."

The Mileses were elated, and just as unbelieving as Cheri and I had been.

"I just can't believe it," said Mrs. Miles. "She's . . . dying . . . and she wanted to get up—got up!"

They asked for all the details. Eric and Kevin got on the extension to hear. A weird state of euphoria set in. Maybe Riann would live forever. That kind of feeling.

Eight thousand miles away, the Easter morning sun was rising in the Holy Land. And it was, for us, in that moment, as if Riann's spirit was taking over . . . as if she was showing us . . .

"the ultimate meaning of that prodigious spiritual energy born of the Cross. . . . A growth of spirit arising from a deficiency of matter. A possible Christification of suffering. This is indeed the miracle which has been constantly renewed for the last two thousand years."

[From *L'Energie spirituelle de la souffrance* by Pierre Teilhard de Chardin, as quoted and translated by Christopher F. Mooney, *Teilhard de Chardin and the Mystery of Christ* (New York: Harper & Row, 1966), p. 114.]

26.

I don't remember much about that Easter other than that I didn't go to church. I have always looked forward to Easter for a conglomeration of reasons. But coming home in a cab that Easter Sunday just after noon, seeing all the people walking home from church, hearing the bells . . . It was like watching a movie.

I slept a long, long time—until about 11:00 P.M. Then I got up for an hour or so, and went right back to sleep.

Monday I packed fresh night clothes and went to the office. At some point I had talked with Paul, told him what was happening. He told me not to worry, to come to the office when I could and go to the hospital when I had to. He knew I would do my work sooner or later.

Mrs. Miles telephoned me at the office once or twice. Riann had had an all right night, but not great. I told her I would be at Children's about five-thirty. That's about when Mr. Miles would get there, too, she said, and they'd leave for Rock Shores soon after.

When I arrived, Riann was lying on the daybed. It was a change of "scene," and, I think, a bit softer than her own bed. Riann was very, very thin. I have no idea how much she weighed, but it couldn't have been much.

She was having her "dinner"—soup, Coke, ice cream and cherry jello. But a couple of bites of soup and the jello were the only things she had eaten.

Mrs. Miles explained that Riann had been so uncomfortable very early that morning that they had decided to try the daybed.

"And Mommy slept in my bed," Riann giggled.

"Yes," laughed Mrs. Miles. "And you'll never guess what my dear, sweet, little daughter said!"

Riann giggled again.

"What?" I asked.

"I asked Ri what would happen if Dr. Verdi came in and found me in her bed," said Mrs. Miles. "And my love over there said, 'Oh, that's all right, Mommy; he could just do brain surgery on you!' "

"Riann!" I exclaimed, playing along. "Your poor mother!"

"Well," said Riann with a half-laugh, "all I know is he's not going to do it on me any more! Two times is enough!"

Yes, we agreed, two times is quite enough.

I could see that Mrs. Miles's nerves had scraped each other raw. The teasing and laughing, done for Riann's sake, had become higher pitched.

Mr. Miles arrived and I went to the cafeteria with some nurses for dinner. When I returned, the Mileses were ready to go.

"If there's any change, call," said Mrs. Miles as I walked with them down the hall. "And can you call around ten, regardless?"

"Sure, don't worry, I'll call."

"I didn't get much sleep last night . . . And I have a feeling you didn't either, on Friday and Saturday. Are you sure you still want to do this?"

"I'm sure."

"Well, we do feel better with you here. Dr. Verdi is amazed it has lasted this long . . ."

"Life has been happy for Riann," I said. "She's not eager to give it up. And that's a tribute to you two, to your family . . ."

Riann was in a good mood that Monday. She was still seizing, but not quite as often and not losing consciousness. Her tongue was raw, however, and giving her a lot of pain. We tried salves, but they didn't help much. (Of all the stupid things: dying of a brain tumor and having so much pain from your tongue, rubbed raw from seizing. Grief.)

There was a note for me on Riann's bulletin board. It was from

Dr. Jenssen. She said Riann told her that when I had spent the night with her Saturday I had put some rollers in my hair, and that I "looked funny."

"Riann! This note from Dr. Jenssen says you told her I look funny with rollers in my hair! Shame on you!"

Giggle. Giggle. "Well, that's what you said, too."

"Well, I guess I did. But, gee, you didn't have to tell Dr. Jenssen!" I laughed.

"I wore curlers once . . . for my first communion."

"I saw that picture. Your hair was curled. You looked very pretty."

"Thank you. It was nice, my first communion . . . just before I got sick."

"Was that Natalie with you?" Natalie was Riann's cousin, next-door neighbor, and best friend next to her sister, Allison.

"Yes. She was in the picture you saw. We went together . . .

"You know, I don't know what to eat first when I get home. Mommy says we can go to the Japanese Village, too. I love it there!"

"Well, I'm sure you're not going to want any more cherry jello!"

"No, but I like it here. It tastes good."

"Do you want some now?"

"No, thank you, but maybe later."

"OK."

Riann was becoming less and less comfortable. She asked—always politely, but with great pain in her eyes and voice—to have her pillows "fixed" every fifteen or twenty minutes. After about three or four "pillow fixes" I knew, and she knew, that the only thing that would help would be to turn her. But it was *so* painful, so very, very painful.

By early Easter Sunday morning, with permission from the

nurses, I had started turning her myself rather than call for help each time. Her mother had done the same. There was simply no medical trick to it. It was going to hurt, agonize, no matter what.

. And Riann really couldn't help much in the turn. The only things she could move were her arms and hands, and even they were becoming stiff. Her neck and head were bent back farther and farther, nearer to the small of her back than to her chest. Her knees were buckled up as far as they would go. Her mouth was chapped and sore and her body was covered with red marks from her thinly covered bones rubbing against the mattress.

But strange as this may sound, she was still beautiful. No, not just because I loved her. In all that pain, she was still beautiful, outside as well as inside. Her clear blue eyes had become huge— partly because her face was getting thinner and partly because her pupils were dilating (a sign of impending death). Her hair seemed thicker and her cheeks were pink.

But turning her, that was a problem. No, it didn't hurt her mother and me—literally hurt us—as it hurt Riann. But figuratively it did.

By late that Monday night, there was no way even to touch her, let alone turn her, without causing great pain. Yet, the pain from *not* being touched, not being turned, must have been greater still.

This particular time I had spent five minutes trying to "fix" her pillows, a large one and a small one. But it wasn't working. We knew . . .

"Ri, should I turn you?"

"Can we try the pillows just once more?"

"Sure, sweetheart, as many times as you want."

But it didn't work. Her face had that look of resigned fear, and I bit my lip. I was having trouble steeling my nerves for another turn, too.

"Ri, why don't I ask your nurse to turn you this time. Maybe she can do it better than me."

"OK."

I walked toward the door to call the nurse.

"Nina . . ."

"Yes, sweetheart?"

". . . not to be mean . . ."

I turned back and kissed her. "Riann, you couldn't be mean if you tried! When you hurt less, I hurt less. You haven't hurt my feelings!" I kissed her again. "I'll be right back with Cheri."

Once again, Riann had been unbelievable. In that much pain, and she had worried that she had hurt my feelings, had been "mean" by asking that her nurse try to turn her. Unbelievable.

Cheri turned Riann the next two or three times.

It was an hour or so later. ". . . Maybe you'd better turn me again."

"I'll get Cheri."

"Nina, you can do it. It doesn't make any difference."

"Are you sure? Cheri doesn't mind."

"I know, but it doesn't matter."

My stomach started to knot again. It's awful to try to help someone and know you're hurting them at the same time. I had been glad Cheri was turning her.

"It's going to hurt, you know . . ."

"Yes . . . I know . . ."

I had to laugh. "That was a kind of stupid thing for me to say, wasn't it, Ri?! I guess you do know."

Riann laughed a tiny, ironic laugh. "Yes . . ."

I turned her. It hurt. Naturally.

There really wasn't any medicine that would help Riann's pain beyond what she was already getting. The doctors tried, but nothing else helped much. Even her seizure medication didn't keep her from seizing. Other than simply drugging her out, there was nothing that could be done.

About midnight Riann decided she was "ready to go to sleep." Cheri came and put her back into bed from the daybed, again with much pain. We "fixed" her pillows and I turned out all but the night light.

"Do you want to try to say prayers, Riann?"

"Yes, that would be nice. Maybe I can make it . . ."

She had been seizing so much on Easter Sunday morning that all we had tried was the "Our Father," and even then she had had a seizure right in the middle of it. But she went on anyway, trying to finish the prayer. I told her God would understand. (A person ought to be able to get through the Lord's Prayer without seizing . . .)

"Do you want to go first?" I asked.

"OK. Dear God, thank you for a nice day. And it was a nice day, even if I was a little sick. God bless Allison and Kevin and Eric and Mommy and Daddy and Grandma and all my friends. Please make my tongue stop hurting. Please make me better so I can get out of here. I'm so happy that I got ten dollars from my cousin and an Easter basket. Even if I didn't get to the Easter egg roll or have Easter . . ."

She opened her eyes—the signal that it was my turn. I prayed. Then we said the "Our Father." Made it! No seizures!

Riann awakened more often Monday night than she had Friday or Saturday nights. But she did get some sleep. Once she awakened and wanted to play a game—"I spy." And another time, as the sun was coming up, she wanted me to read her the funny papers. I guess something reminded her of a Sunday morning at home.

At about 6:30 A.M. she and I both fell asleep, for over a whole hour! The neurosurgeons stuck their heads in on morning rounds at about 7:45, but I just pulled the sheet over my face.

Later, as I was drinking coffee at the nursing station and Riann was still asleep, Dr. Craig teased, "You certainly sleep late! What do you think this is, a hotel?" Dr. Craig came very close to having hot coffee all over his long, straggly brown hair and long, straggly brown moustache!

"You know what's happening, I think," he added. "Riann's getting her nights and days mixed. It happens a lot."

"Goody," I said. "Thanks for telling me. You're a delight first thing in the morning!"

"I know."

27.

I thought Riann was going to die Wednesday night. She was so sick. Not only was she seizing more often—at least every fifteen minutes—and not only was she in more pain, but now she could barely swallow and her lungs were full of mucus.

Her mother said that between seizures she had slept most of the day. And, true to Dr. Craig's prediction, she was awake most of the night. She could barely talk, and didn't much—just to ask about her pillow and turning.

They brought in a suction machine and suctioned her two or three times, but the pain must have been great each time. Once she was able to cough up a tremendous amount of thick, ugly, green-black mucus by herself. I was alone with her. I held Kleenex and held her head and encouraged her to keep coughing. It was awful—and my description is mild. But she really got a lot out.

If anyone had told me before the fact that I could have gone through this I never would have believed them. My stomach was sick for a long, long time. But Riann seemed to feel better.

It worried her that she couldn't swallow. She would try to eat cherry jello, but it would just stay in her mouth and squish around her teeth. Finally she gave up.

She didn't sleep all night. Neither did I. I was scared, really really scared.

But morning came. And Riann managed to swallow some soup.

I went to work, and counted the minutes until five o'clock, when I went home and slept.

Friday night she was better. She still had her days and nights mixed, still was awake all night. But this time she was more comfortable—relatively speaking. The seizures had lessened again, or maybe we were just accepting them more. Her tongue hurt less, or maybe it had just developed calluses?

She could swallow better, though her swallowing had a funny sound.

"It sounds like I'm swallowing bones . . . like a goat," she joked one time. It did, actually.

At three in the morning, just after a move from the bed to the daybed, we decided to read stories. Her neck was hurting. Maybe a story would take her mind off it.

We read—I read aloud—about "Flat Stanley," who somehow managed to become flat, which was nice because he didn't have to watch his weight and he could fit between the grating in the pavement to retrieve a ring his mother had dropped. But it wasn't so nice, either, because sometimes people laughed at him. However, true to all such stories, something wonderful happened and Flat Stanley became round again.

"Flat Stanley" was a funny story and Riann giggled a lot throughout. I hated for it to end. I read some others, but none was as funny as "Flat Stanley."

Later, back in bed, Riann looked over at the window ledge. Clive the Bookworm and Mrs. McPatches were sitting there, kind of facing each other. "Nina, look . . . Clive and Mrs. McPatches are getting to know each other." She giggled. It did look funny.

"You know, the other night, when you weren't here, I woke up and saw Clive in the middle of the night. I remembered that story you wrote about when Clive wanted to become a neurosurgeon. I pretended to picture him in the operating room saying, 'Give me a knife. Give me this . . .' That was a funny story." Giggle. Giggle.

Finally, at six A.M., she fell asleep. Me too. At eight o'clock Dr. Craig stuck his head around the door, saw me still in bed, and went, "Tsk, tsk." I stuck out my tongue, and pulled the sheets over my head.

It was Saturday morning, so I didn't have to go to the office.

I was up and dressed by nine. Riann awakened as I was straightening the daybed.

"Do you think you can sleep any more?" I asked, ready to get her breakfast if the answer was no.

"No, but I think I'll just loll in bed for a while."

"OK," I smiled. "You tell me when you want breakfast."

"I will."

She fell asleep again.

I went to the nursing station for coffee. I was really tired, and not quite as awake as I had thought. As I sat in the back room with my feet up and my second cup of coffee in hand, looking out toward the hallway, I saw a huge yellow bird walk by.

I put down the coffee cup with both hands and rubbed my eyes. It was still there. "I'm losing my mind," I figured. Then I realized that it was Big Bird from the "Sesame Street" television program. He and several other "Sesame Street" characters had come to visit the children. I had to laugh at myself.

I went back to Riann's room. She opened her eyes as I went in. "Ri, do you ever watch 'Sesame Street'?"

"Sure."

"Well, I just saw Big Bird in the hallway. He's come to visit. Would you like to see him?"

"Yes! Please!"

"OK, I'll be right back."

I found Big Bird at the other end of the hall. I asked if he could come to room 381. I explained that Riann was "pretty sick," but that he could talk with her and ask her questions . . . just please not be too loud.

He was great. And Riann loved it. It really perked her up.

Then she asked me to pull down the window shade and she went back to sleep. After all, it was her night now.

I went to the cafeteria with one of the nurses for a cup of coffee.

When I returned, Riann's day nurse was giving her a thorough bed bath and changing her nightgown. That had to hurt. I couldn't watch. I was chicken. She couldn't have been that dirty. Why not let her alone? But I didn't know this nurse. I couldn't say anything.

When I saw the nurse leave, I went back in. Riann was lying on the daybed and she looked more beautiful than any time I saw her during those last days. She had on a very feminine little blue nightgown that matched her blue eyes perfectly. Her cheeks were pink and her lips were washed clean of the dried mucus. She did look much better . . . but she didn't feel better. I still don't know if it was worth it.

"Riann, you look so pretty!"

"I don't feel pretty . . ."

"I know, sweetheart. It's miserable being back here again, isn't it?"

"It sure is. You know, Nina, I wish I could just snap my fingers and make it all go away . . ."

"I wish you could, too, Ri . . . I wish you could too . . ."

Saturday night I had an actual date! Nothing big, just dinner, a long, long dinner. But it was nice, so nice.

Sunday morning I went to church. Dr. Davies was preaching. It was like a shot in the arm.

"You look pale," he said after church. "And where were you last Sunday? I didn't see you."

"Riann Miles is dying. I've been spending some time with her."

"You watch it! You're too involved."

"Yes, but I love Riann. Why, how it happened, I don't know. But it's very hard not to love her, for anyone who meets her."

"Well, watch it!"

"Yes, sir."

We didn't talk farther about it. But I could tell in his eyes he understood.

He'll die, I realized once again, as I walked out into the blinding Sunday sunlight . . . long, long before I die, very likely. Will he ever know how much he's given me, in his sermons, in our long discussions? Will he ever realize how many sheep he's fed?

> Are not all lifelong friendships born at the moment when at last you meet another human being who has some inkling . . . of that something which you were born desiring, and which, beneath the flux of other desires and in all the momentary silences between the louder passions, night and day, year by year, from childhood to old age, you are looking for, watching for, listening for?
>
> [From *The Problem of Pain* by C. S. Lewis. Copyright 1944 by The Macmillan Co. and used by permission.]

I went to brunch with David, who yelled at me, as usual. Good old David.

On Tuesday, a depression came over Riann. Her nights were still her days. The pains were still there. The seizures were still there. The fact that, for all practical purposes, she couldn't move had begun to set in . . .

"I don't know why she [the nurse] worried about putting the side of the bed up, I can't roll off . . . I can't move! Oh, I want to go home . . ."

It was said, that last sentence, with a hesitancy, a tone that said, "I know it will never be." Maybe that was my imagination. Maybe it was just that I had never heard Riann that depressed before, though I had often reminded her that she could feel free to tell me exactly how she felt, that she didn't have to "put on a happy front" if she didn't feel that way.

But nonetheless, the old fear came back that Tuesday. What

if she asks *The Question?* What can I say?

Finally, I got up my courage. In all fairness, maybe she wants to talk, to get out how upset she is. Just don't let her ask The Question, please, God . . .

"You know, Riann, I've said before that I want you to complain whenever you want to with me. Anyone in the hospital has a perfect right to be in a bad mood now and then. I'm glad when you're in a good mood, mind you, but with Mommy and Daddy and me, we want you to tell us exactly how you feel, no matter what. OK?"

"OK."

"And Riann, today you sound awfully depressed, unhappy. Are you?"

" . . . Yes. I just wish I didn't have this neck problem. It bothers me like crazy."

"I know it does, Ri. It doesn't seem fair, does it?"

"No . . . You know, when I was in the hospital before, I got so many stuffed animals . . . Mommy said someday we could give some to the poor . . . there are so many . . ."

At that moment the neurosurgeons came in on rounds. Riann's was their last room. I walked out with Dr. McMahan. "You know, I'm afraid Riann knows she's dying."

"Why?"

"Well, first of all, she's more depressed than I've ever seen her, which, of course, she has reason to be. And then, just as you guys were coming in, she commented on how, when she was here before, people sent her presents . . ."

"Sure, the old 'Dying Child Syndrome.' People are afraid to send cards and gifts . . . afraid they'll arrive 'after the fact.' A bright kid like Riann can figure that out fast . . . or at least begin to wonder."

Later, on the telephone, I told Mrs. Miles about Riann's comment and Dr. McMahan's comment. She said the next day she would bring some things to brighten the room and hang some cards. It made sense. Or, it fed the denial. I'm not sure which. Maybe both.

But Riann still didn't ask The Question. Maybe we should have given her more chance. But I know I was too scared. Now, maybe I wouldn't be. I don't know. But then I was.

Tuesday night rivaled the previous Wednesday for Riann's lack of comfort. In desperation I probably asked Mary Katharine Soloman—who was a super-kind, perceptive, and understanding nurse —at least five times for something to help Riann's pain. Anything! Usually, Mary Katharine just came and turned Riann or stood by her for a little while . . . or stood by me. Anyway, I was grateful for Mary Katharine that night.

All night long, every five or ten minutes, I would "fix" Riann's pillows, stand by her bedside to make sure it had worked, then tiptoe back to the daybed and slip under the sheets. At times I would pray that she would sleep—for just thirty minutes uninterrupted. Pray as much for my sake as hers. Now, it sounds selfish. Then, it was for sanity.

But the "fixed" pillows would last only five minutes . . .

"Nina . . ." Very softly.

"Yes, sweetheart?"

"I'm sorry, but my neck . . . my pillows . . ."

"It's all right, Riann. You call any time, sweetheart. I mean that. I don't mind. The most important thing is for you to be comfortable."

"Thank you."

It was the most important thing. That's why I jumped up each time without hesitation. But it didn't keep me from dreading to hear the call, gripping my fingernails into my flesh, trying to race to see if my muscles and nerves could relax even the slightest before she would call again.

But she couldn't help it. I kept reminding myself. I would have months to rest, years to relax my muscles. Who would I rather be in those moments of pain, Riann or me? That was the question that kept me going. For her, now was the rest of her life. For me, it was a few nights of no sleep. The comparison—that's what did it.

"Nina . . ."

This time it took an hour. One hour. And I'm not exaggerating in the least. One hour of "fixing" the pillows, turning her, moving her to the daybed and then back to bed. Nothing was working. I wanted to scream. I'm sure Riann did, too.

Finally, we hit the right combination. Her relief was genuine. "That's it! That's it, that's perfect! Thank you."

"Good, fantastic!" I kissed her and stood there a moment. But she didn't say, "No, wait a minute . . . could you please try again . . ." All was quiet.

I crept back to the daybed. Slipped under the covers.

"Nina . . ."

Oh, no . . . no . . . Oh, no . . . "Yes, Riann?"

"Have a good night's sleep."

Friday I had to go to New Jersey. I had known all along I would have to go.

An emeritus professor from my divinity school, Professor Beaver, was now director of a missionary study center near Atlantic City. He had asked me to speak at a seminar. The center would pay my way.

I had planned the mini-vacation well. First, from Friday evening until Monday morning, I was going to visit close friends, Nancy and John Miller, in Morristown, New Jersey, where John is pastor of the Presbyterian church. Then Dr. and Mrs. Beaver were going to pick me up in Morristown and drive me to their home. I was to speak there Tuesday, then go home to Maryland on Wednesday to visit my parents through the weekend.

I had been looking forward to it. It would be good to see my parents, and, I hoped, my Aunt Helen and Uncle "Doc"; and good to have a long talk with Nancy, my dearest friend, who had moved to Morristown just as I was beginning my chaplaincy. I was anxious to see their children, Amy and Andrew—how they'd grown!—and even their dog, Bambi. Something normal. A reminder of the rest of the world.

My involvement with Riann was deep. But I realized my limits. Staying in the Midwest, canceling my plans, wouldn't have given her life, wouldn't have made her well. I had done what I could when I could. If she was still alive when I returned, still aware, I likely would spend every other night with her again, just the same. I could do that. It wasn't killing me.

But going to New Jersey and Maryland, as planned, was the right thing to do. On one condition: if Riann died, I wanted to return for her funeral. Her parents understood that. They agreed without question to telephone me if Riann died while I was gone.

So Thursday was to be my last night with Riann, for a while at least. And, all things considered, it was a good one. Compared with Tuesday, it was fantastic.

Riann's depression seemed to have gone. Maybe it was decorating her room with cards and some flowers and balloons . . . Maybe the tumor had moved to a better spot . . . Maybe Riann had asked God *The Question* and together they had gotten it resolved . . . I don't know. But I do know she was in much better spirits. Still in pain, but in much better spirits.

A note from her mother said Riann had been awake a good bit that day. "Maybe you can get some sleep tonight!"

I had my suitcase with me. Mrs. Miles and her sister, Meg, who had come in from New England the past week, had insisted on driving me to the airport so I could have as much time as possible with Riann on Friday.

I went downstairs with some nurses for coffee. Riann had been asleep when I arrived and was still asleep when I returned from downstairs. I changed into my nightclothes and read.

"Nina . . ."

"Hi, sleepyhead! How do you feel?" It was about 10:15 P.M.

"OK. May I have some cherry jello, please?"

I laughed. "You know, they've had to hire a special cook just to make cherry jello . . . to keep up with you!"

She hadn't been eating much. A few bites at each meal. I anticipated the same this time.

But she didn't stop eating and she didn't stop talking for two solid hours. She went through nearly two tubs of cherry jello—which was monumental—and her whole life's history.

They say people relive their whole life in their mind before they die. I didn't think about it that night, but that may have been exactly what Riann was doing. Whatever it was, I heard about experiences in all of her nine years, from as far back as she could remember.

"I remember . . . there's this boy . . . his name is Henry Alexander . . . when we were babies . . . there's this picture of him kissing me . . . so everybody teases me and says he's my boyfriend. He's not . . . but they tease me. I remember riding in a car pool with Henry one time . . . and I hid so people wouldn't see us together.

"And one time I went swimming and Henry was going to be there . . . and I had these two bathing suits . . . one was a bikini and the other just a regular halter . . . and I decided to wear the regular one . . . so people wouldn't say I was wearing the bikini for Henry.

"I have two boyfriends now—at least two! One is John McArthur . . . he makes a funny sound with his mouth. I love to see him do it. He makes me laugh. He makes everybody laugh. He's so funny. I think he's handsome, too. I'll try to make the sound, but I'm not as good as John . . ."

She tried, really tried. She could barely move her facial muscles and her arms and hands, which were also required for the "funny sound." The procedure involved putting her index fingers into her mouth. Finally, she succeeded as best she could.

"That's kind of it," she said. "But I'm not as good as John. You should hear him!"

I laughed. "As far as I'm concerned, you're pretty good! That is a funny sound. No wonder John makes you laugh."

She giggled. "He really does. He's so funny."

"Allison has a boyfriend, too. Though I don't know if she likes him as much as he likes her. He gave her a present at Christmas. It was pretty . . . a ring.

"Her birthday is coming soon. I'm making her some needlepoint. Mommy has been helping me. Maybe we can work on it tomorrow . . . I want to have it done by her birthday. I hope I can . . .

"You know, I did something I shouldn't have once . . . I guess. But I don't think Daddy would get mad. You see, I get ten cents allowance and Daddy gives it to me every Friday. But sometimes he's in a hurry and I'm afraid he's going to forget. Well, this one time I kind of reminded him as he was going out the door. He reached in his pocket and gave me a quarter. I guess he didn't have a dime. I was going to say something, but then I decided not to . . ."

When she stopped talking and said she had had enough cherry jello it was nearly 12:30 A.M. The nursing shifts had changed and we hadn't even known it.

I turned out the light, kissed her good-night, and she slept for three hours . . . slept right through her seizures. And even after that, she only got awake five or six times. I couldn't believe the change.

And, you know, we really had fun those two hours of talking. I forgot for moments that we weren't just at home having some dessert and relaxing. The mind can be a great protector . . .

If this had to be the last night I spent with her—and it was—at least it was a "good" one, a fun one . . . all things considered.

When I returned to Children's from the office
that Friday it was about 12:45 p.m. My plane was to leave at 3:30;
so we were going to leave the hospital about 2:30.

I ran into Mrs. Miles and her sister as I got off the bus in back
of the hospital. They were on their way back from lunch. We
went to Riann's room. Dr. Jenssen was with her. Riann loved Dr.
Jenssen, and the feeling was returned deeply. Riann was lying on
the daybed. Dr. Jenssen was showing her some red clogs she had
ordered for her from Sweden.

Dr. Jenssen had been upset earlier because the clogs had taken
so long to get here—like the beanbag chair. She was afraid to give
them to Riann this late.

"Go ahead," Mrs. Miles had said. "She'll love them! Really she
will. She won't mind that she can't use them right away. Just
having them, seeing them, will be enough. And red is her favorite
color."

Riann did like the clogs. They made her happy. She showed
them to me when I came in.

"They're great, Riann; and I love the color!"

"Yes, me too."

She was buried wearing them.

Mrs. Miles and her sister and I sat and talked
with Riann for a while. Then Mrs. Miles and her sister went "to
get a cup of coffee."

They were leaving us alone to say good-bye. It was thoughtful
of them. But neither of us could. If we knew it would be our last
time together we didn't let on. And I think we knew.

We kissed good-bye, and she whispered, "Have a good trip
. . . I love you . . ."

There is so much I have told you—all of it true,
none "made-up" to convey mood. But there is so much I haven't

told you—not on purpose, but because exact memory fails me.

Mrs. Miles and I had many long conversations—survival conversations, detail conversations, emotional conversations, plain ordinary conversations. She was suffering far more than I have been able to relate. So was Mr. Miles; but somehow I always felt inadequate to "minister" to him. I guess part of me still figured I needed to be a priest. And part of him was still in shock.

If you have become a bit impatient in these last pages, that was my desire. Dying—*real life dying*—is not like the movies. It can take longer than expected. Riann lived eighteen days beyond that Holy Thursday. It can become routine—frighteningly routine. And it is not pretty: Seizures, mucus, pain . . . they are not glossed over in real life dying, and they *purposely* were not glossed over here.

Yet for all my description of Riann's pain, her discomfort, I haven't begun to convey its magnitude. What I have conveyed, I hope, is her sense of humor, her outlook, her hope, her faith, her love, her "hanging in there" that remained constant to the end.

I wasn't soothing the Mileses when I said Riann loved life and wanted to hang onto it as long as possible . . . and that was a tribute to their family. I meant it. I sincerely believe that home and family was so wonderful for Riann, and that she felt so secure in her parents' love and her brothers' and sister's love, that she couldn't even imagine that anything could permanently separate her from "home." "Home" and "love" were synonymous for Riann.

Perhaps that is why she may not have been afraid to die.

> Love bears all things, believes all things, hopes all things, endures all things. Love never ends.
>
> [1 Corinthians 13:7–8]

It was Monday night. I was in New Jersey. The professor and his wife and I had just returned from dinner. It was an enjoyable evening.

Mrs. Miles had said when they dropped me at the airport Friday that either she or her sister would telephone me on Monday evening to give me a "progress report."

So when the telephone rang and it was Mrs. Miles, that's what I expected.

"It happened. This morning at ten o'clock. She died."

I wasn't prepared. I didn't know what to say.

She went on. She told me the whole story. I know I didn't move. The professor and his wife could tell by my face. Kindly, they left me alone.

Dr. Praeder had looked in on Riann at about seven-thirty that morning. He checked her briefly and gave her a kiss. Riann had teased Dr. Praeder in the past because he didn't kiss hard enough.

"How is that?" he asked as he gave her a big kiss.

"That was hard enough!" Riann replied.

At nine that morning she went into a seizure. But this time she lost consciousness, went into a coma.

Her day nurse called Mary Cooke.

"Call her parents and call the doctors. It doesn't look good."

Mary stayed with Riann from then on . . . until she died, about an hour later.

It had been Mary Cooke who had said to me that Saturday sixteen days before, when Riann got her first seizure, "I pray to

God I won't be here when she dies. I don't want that. Anything but that." But at 10 A.M. that Monday, Mary Cooke was there. And she was the only one who was there.

Riann's mother and father couldn't physically get there in time.

Dr. Verdi was giving a seminar at University Medical School.

Dr. Jenssen was taking some medical exams in a nearby suburb.

And I was in New Jersey . . . mailing Riann a postcard.

Ironic, wasn't it? Mrs. Miles was to say that time and again afterwards. "It must have been God's plan," she would say. "None of those who were closest to Riann were there when she died."

I don't know if it was God's plan or not. But I'm glad I didn't have to see Riann dead. I'm glad the last things I remember about Riann are "Have a good trip . . . I love you . . ." and how beautiful she looked that Saturday morning in her blue nightgown. They are better memories than seeing her dead, I think.

Mrs. Miles continued on the telephone late on that Monday night. The funeral was to be Wednesday afternoon at a Catholic church in Rock Shores. The church where the Mileses were members.

"But Nina, Riann had such a beautiful 'last day' on Sunday, with the whole family. The children came in—even Kevin, though it was awfully hard for him. Dr. Verdi talked with him a long time—man-to-man—and it helped a lot.

"And Riann was so good, so very good. It was a good 'last day.' I'll always be grateful for that."

I think I knew what she meant. I was grateful for the "good" last night I had had with Riann. Things like that are not to be taken lightly. They're important. They're part of the memory that lives on . . . after the bad memories, the mental picture slides, of pain and seizures fade away.

I gave my talk the next day before the assembled missionaries and flew home that same evening . . . home for Riann's funeral.

I could end these writings with details of Riann's funeral; or with what happened after the funeral; or with how Mr. Miles has grown to accept the fact of Riann's death and become able to talk openly about his feelings; or with how the Miles family has grown even closer; or with how I still can't say the Lord's Prayer, the "Our Father," without thinking of Riann; or with how I wouldn't trade the unique gift of knowing Riann Miles in living and dying for any other experience of my life, except one . . .

I could end these writings with a discussion of the theological mystery of pain and death.

All would have validity.

But I shall end it by telling you how I felt on the first anniversary of Riann's death.

I had been on edge for several days. I don't know if it was because of that or not. But I do know on the first anniversary of Riann's death I had to go to her gravesite. I didn't rationalize why or worry about whether or not it was healthy. I just knew I had to go.

I was back working at University Children's, as an advanced student chaplain. I told Craig Hatfield that I was thinking about leaving for a few hours, told him where I wanted to go.

He seemed to understand. "Sometimes we have to bury people again."

Maybe he was right. I don't know if that's what I had to do with Riann or not.

Maybe never having seen her dead, I hadn't buried her in the first place. Though I'm not sure that's it, either.

Regardless, I went. And I sat on Riann's tombstone for an hour and a half. It seemed like ten minutes. And I had a wrestling match with God.

I was claiming "me," crying out, "My God, my God, why hast thou forsaken me?" Yes, I knew better. But yes, I was justified. Anger is a reality, a human reality, in real relationship with God.

In those moments, sitting on Riann's tombstone, I was claiming the intensity of my being . . . and claiming God's love in the same breath.

That evening I wrote this:

> Some theologian or another once described ministry as "one person's attempt to give God's answers to men's questions." Or, to put it another way, one person's attempt to answer the unanswerable.
>
> Today I sat on a tombstone alone in a small cemetery and had a long talk with God. I told him I was figuring out that the child beneath the tombstone really was dead: Not first "in God's arms" or "seeing his face" or "alive in his heart" or "one with him." But first and foremost and above all, she was dead. Had been dead for 365 days and three hours. And I couldn't talk with her anymore. And I couldn't hold her. And it wasn't fair . . . or rational . . . or answerable . . . or reasonable . . . or very loving, when all was said and done, by a God I kept calling "love."
>
> The only *real* thing I knew as I sat on that tombstone— knew firmly, gut-level, for the first time—was that that child was dead.
>
> What sham we feed these people! I hurled at God. You're second-best . . . the crutch . . . the aspirin to ease the pain of nevermore. You're the lost future—better than no future. You're the hope unseen that beats no hope. Eschatology—fantastic word!
>
> All these people who sit in small waiting rooms and shake on plexiglass chairs and wait for someone to tell them it's not true. Their child is alive. That's what they want to hear. "It was a mistake." Or, "There's been a miracle. He's alive!"
>
> So what do I do . . . minister . . . reverend person? I tell them he's alive. Oh, he's dead all right. But he's "seeing God's face" or he's "in God's arms" or he "won't have to suffer any more pain." Check out Revelation: No pain, no sorrow, no darkness. Whee!
>
> But sitting on that tombstone, I couldn't tell God where to go. I couldn't tell him to leave me alone. Was I too scared, worried

about my insurance policy? I am a kind of chicken. Was I not hurt *enough?* Could I have renounced God if it had been my own child, my very own child beneath the tombstone with the recent rainwater oozing and bubbling over the naked rectangle? Was this the biggie test of faith? My freedom-to-reject being tested to make my freedom-to-accept more real?

　　　Maybe. Maybe not. Maybe there is no God. Maybe he has sold out and left town. Or maybe the strict fundamentalists are right . . . or the Hindus . . . or the Buddhists . . . or the atheists. Maybe the Maharaj Ji is it?

When I got that far, I stopped.

　　　Yes, it is unanswerable. Yes, I am going right on attempting to answer it. That's ministry to me.

　　　The unanswerable has many faces: faith, hope, prayer, sacrament, revelation . . .

　　　The attempt to answer has many faces: words, no words, caring, touching, worship, silence, strength, weakness, sharing . . .

　　　All I *know* is I'm not alone. But I sure am curious about the nature of the Being who walks with me. And I guess I'll never really be happy being human . . . despite the lip service . . . until I get my unanswerables answered . . .

Of course, I won't . . . on this Earth . . . get my unanswerables answered. So, as I see it, this moment, it's my choice.

Today I choose God. I hope forever. I know anger will come back . . . and frustration . . . and fear . . .

But I know I'll never be alone.

And that is everything.

　　　All through life's day we shall walk with the Christ, often as the Stranger, because He never obtrudes or overrides. Before the journey's end we shall ask many questions, experience many heartaches, be molded by many of life's disciplining disappointments.

And then, suddenly, whether we shall be young, middleaged, or old we shall find that the day is far spent, that the shadows are gathering and at last the night descends. In that moment our eyes shall be opened and we shall know Him, but now no longer as One who will vanish from our sight, but as the living, traveling Companion along the unknown valley's way to the highroad of God's eternity. Then shall come to pass the saying, "Death is swallowed up in victory" (I Corinthians 15:54, RSV).

[From *This Side of Eden* by Elam Davies. © 1964 by Fleming H. Revell Co. and used by permission.]

Riann and I had given each other the same gift one time. Mine from her sits still on my office desk: a small, wooden, orange-and-black ladybug attached to a clothespin. Hers from me sits still on her bed next to the window in Rock Shores: a large, stuffed, orange-and-black ladybug.

Out of the muddy ground that April afternoon . . . where spring's grass was being made . . . from the crevice next to the chilled marble tombstone, came a tiny ladybug marching toward me. I put my finger in its path and lifted it up.

It marched forward, undaunted.

Not the End